SPECTACULAR
BRITAIN

CONWAY
Bloomsbury Publishing Plc
50 Bedford Square, London, WC1B 3DP, UK
29 Earlsfort Terrace, Dublin 2, Ireland

BLOOMSBURY, CONWAY and the
Conway logo are trademarks of Bloomsbury
Publishing Plc

First published in Great Britain 2024

For legal purposes the Acknowledgements
on page 288 constitute an extension of this
copyright page

The publisher and author cannot accept
responsibility for any errors or omissions in
this book, or loss, injury or inconvenience
arising from use of this book.

This book is a guide for when you spend time
outdoors. Undertaking any activity outdoors
or at night carries with it some risks that
cannot be entirely eliminated. For example,
you might get lost on a route or caught in bad
weather. Before you spend time outdoors,
we therefore advise that you always take the
necessary precautions, such as checking
weather forecasts and ensuring that you have
all the equipment you need. Any walking
routes that are described in this book
should not be relied upon as a sole means of
navigation, so we recommend that you check
tidal predictions and refer to an Ordnance
Survey map or authoritative equivalent.

A catalogue record for this book is
available from the British Library
Library of Congress Cataloguing-in-
Publication data has been applied for

ISBN: PB: 978-1-8448-6634-2;
ePub: 978-1-8448-6635-9;
ePDF: 978-1-8448-6636-6

10 9 8 7 6 5 4 3 2 1

Typeset in Spectral
Designed by Austin Taylor
Printed in Malaysia by
  Papercraft Ltd

MIX
Paper | Supporting
responsible forestry
FSC™ C007207

To find out more about our authors
and books visit www.bloomsbury.com
and sign up for our newsletters

SPECTACULAR BRITAIN

A SPOTTER'S GUIDE TO THE UK'S MOST AMAZING NATURAL PHENOMENA

KEVIN SENE

CONWAY

LONDON · OXFORD · NEW YORK · NEW DELHI · SYDNEY

CONTENTS

Picture credits
PREVIOUS PAGE: Coastal fog at Freshwater Bay, Isle of Wight.
© Getty/s0ulsurfing - Jason Swain
THIS PAGE: Mealt Falls Aurora.
© Getty Images/Ollie Taylor

INTRODUCTION

BACKGROUND

From the Northern Lights to whirling coastal birds, the British Isles experience some of the world's finest natural spectacles. Each has its own band of enthusiasts, drawn by the magic of seeing something truly special and out of the ordinary. Some only occur at certain times of the year, such as tidal bores and the annual deer rut, while others only happen when conditions are right, including sunken villages that reappear and the UK's only named wind. Other examples are lunar eclipses, mountain waves and leaping salmon.

If you are not an expert, though, what are your chances of a sighting? This book aims to help, providing tips on when and where to go and other practical information. A grading system indicates how widespread events are and how often they occur. For example, the Northern Lights are only visible occasionally and are best seen from northern areas so they have a high level of difficulty, while beautiful autumnal colours are a highlight of many woods and parks.

OPPOSITE Les Autelets sea stacks in Sark, site of the largest guillemot colony in the Channel Islands.

BELOW A dramatic cloudscape viewed from the Causeway Coastal Route in Northern Ireland.

NORTHERN LIGHTS

Shetland

Orkney

SALMON RUNS

TIDAL RACES

MOUNTAIN CLOUDS

Scotland

Northern Ireland

AUTUMN COLOURS

RUTTING DEER

LOW TIDE WALKS

NAMED WINDS & WEATHER

Northeast England, Yorkshire & Humberside

Northwest England

WHIRLING WATERBIRDS

SUNKEN VILLAGES

SEABIRD CITIES

East & West Midlands

SEAL PUPS

Wales

East Anglia, London & Southeast England

WILD WATERFALLS

HIDDEN CURRENTS

TIDAL BORES

ECLIPSES & SUPERMOONS

Southwest England

WILDFLOWER DISPLAYS

Channel Islands

METEOR SHOWERS

ABOVE Surfers riding the Severn Bore in Gloucestershire; on the highest tides, large crowds turn out to see the wave pass.

To help improve your chances of a sighting, scientific insights appear throughout. These describe the astronomical, meteorological, ecological and other causes of events. Expert insights appear too, for example from the glider pilots who ride mountain winds and on the joys of watching tidal bores.

When deciding which natural spectacles to include, a key factor was that readers shouldn't require any specialist knowledge or equipment. That is, armed only with a little knowledge and luck, and perhaps a pair of binoculars, most people should have a chance of a sighting. By contrast, the wonderful nature documentaries on television sometimes require weeks of waiting for the perfect moment and expensive camera equipment to capture it.

HOW TO USE THIS GUIDE

Of the many possibilities, this guide includes 18 natural spectacles that non-experts have a reasonable chance of seeing. You can read later about some that nearly made the grade but were just too uncertain to include. Events are grouped under six main headings:

- **Space** – astronomical spectacles occasionally visible in the night sky
- **Weather** – unusual clouds and winds that occur under certain conditions
- **Tides** – unusual sights and walks possible during extreme tides
- **Land** – fleeting flora and wildlife spectacles at some times of year
- **Water** – river, reservoir and coastal spectacles linked to the weather
- **Coast** – extraordinary wildlife sights around the coastline.

NATURAL WONDER OR NATURAL SPECTACLE?

Britain has an extraordinarily diverse range of scenery and habitat. Some sights are truly impressive, such as the Needles on the Isle of Wight and Fingal's Cave in Scotland. Other amazing places include the White Cliffs of Dover, Malham Cove in Yorkshire, the ancient woodlands of Borrowdale in Cumbria, the Giant's Causeway in Northern Ireland and the Cheddar Gorge in Somerset. These are often called natural wonders and – weather and transport permitting – can be visited at any time of year. By contrast, natural spectacles only occur at certain times of year or more rarely, and some require a measure of luck or persistence for a sighting.

RIGHT Fingal's Cave on the Isle of Staffa in the Inner Hebrides has inspired the works of many artists, including the Hebrides Overture 'Fingal's Cave' by Felix Mendelssohn.

BELOW Natural spectacles don't always have to be in remote areas, as illustrated by these fallow deer in Richmond Park in London.

Some spectacles can, of course, be seen in many places – snowdrops, for example – while others require some travel. Maps appear in each section along with 'best of' lists if there is a wide choice of sites. See 'Further reading' too for books, websites and other sources of information that were useful when researching this book.

Given the many uncertainties in predicting natural spectacles, if travelling far perhaps the best attitude is to go in hope but be prepared for disappointment.

Fear not, though, because many spectacles occur in beautiful and wild landscapes, so there are often plenty of interesting places to visit nearby, such as nature reserves and spectacular clifftop walks. You could also try to see more than one type of event on a single trip. For example, spotting waterbirds during a low tide walk or admiring autumn leaves while visiting a deer park.

LEVEL OF DIFFICULTY: THE GRADING SYSTEM

The grading system gives a rough idea of the amount of effort and luck required for a sighting. It is modelled on those used in some climbing, hillwalking and mountain biking guides. Values are on a scale of 1 to 5 stars, based on the following factors:

- **Location** – how widespread is the phenomenon?
- **Frequency** – how often does it occur?
- **Predictability** – how easy is it to predict?
- **Safety** – are there any significant risks to consider?

For example, autumn colours can be seen every year in most towns and cities so they receive a score of ★. On the other hand, the Northern Lights only occur occasionally and may need several attempts before success so they receive a score of ★★★★★. An explanatory note appears where grades vary significantly within a chapter. Values are purely subjective but hopefully give an impression of how easy or difficult a sighting can be. Safety considerations include tidal risks, steep drops, slippery paths, night-time viewing, and the risks of strong winds. For some sights you may need to travel to distant locations, but this aspect is not included in the grades.

NATURAL SPECTACLES: WHAT YOU MIGHT EXPECT TO SEE ON THE BEST DAYS (AND NIGHTS)

	Natural Spectacle	Description
SPACE	**Meteor showers**	Lie back on a warm summer's night and go 'wow' as bright flashes of light pass overhead against a backdrop of stars. Try to spot fireballs on a crisp winter evening.
	Eclipses and supermoons	Marvel as the shadow of the Earth crosses the moon, causing it to darken then glow red. See supermoons rise behind famous landmarks and watch rare partial solar eclipses.
	Northern Lights	Watch in wonder as the horizon starts to glow green, becoming brighter with red or purple pillars shooting into the sky. See mysterious night-shining clouds in summer.
WEATHER	**Hidden currents**	Wonder at the power of a thunderstorm or see mountain peaks poking above a sea of cloud, or mist flowing along a valley when it all calms down.
	Mountain clouds	See mysterious lens-shaped clouds downwind of mountains, with some shaped like flying saucers. Watch a peak gain a helmet or banner of cloud.
	Named winds and weather	Watch a giant cigar-shaped cloud rotate high above a valley and feel the power of the Helm, Britain's only named wind.
TIDES	**Tidal bores**	Admire the power of the tide as a surge speeds inland, sometimes forming breaking waves large enough for a surfer to ride.
	Tidal races	See the powerful waves and eddies formed as the tide races past islands and in and out of lochs, and even one of the world's largest tidal whirlpools.
	Low tide walks	Walk out to a tidal island on a falling tide with rock pools, lighthouses and historic ruins to explore. Cross an ancient route with the King's Guide to the Sands.

	Natural Spectacle	Description
LAND	Autumn colours	Enjoy the spectacular autumn colours of an Atlantic rainforest and the fall colours of the maple without travelling abroad. Visit ancient trees dating from medieval times.
	Wildflower displays	Anticipate the approach of spring as the first snowdrops appear, then walk past carpets of bluebells once it arrives. Marvel at cherry blossoms without having to travel to Japan.
	Rutting deer	See the changes in behaviour of red, fallow, sika and roe deer during the annual deer rut as males intimidate rivals, including an occasional clash of antlers.
WATER	Salmon runs	Spot the flash of salmon as they leap weirs and waterfalls on their annual migration to spawning grounds in the headwaters of rivers.
	Sunken villages	Visit reservoirs when levels are low to see the remains of villages flooded decades ago, and prehistoric forests and footprints around the coast.
	Wild waterfalls	Be amazed as waterfalls flow backwards, produce rainbows, freeze solid or appear out of nowhere, and see beautiful reservoir outflow patterns.
COAST	Whirling waterbirds	Watch the amazing aerobatic displays of wading birds as they twist and turn at high tide or to escape a predator. Observe vast flocks of geese around dawn and dusk.
	Seabird cities	See extraordinary numbers of guillemots, gannets and other seabirds as they balance on cliff ledges to raise their young. Look out for the occasional puffin too.
	Seal pups	Visit islands and secluded bays and beaches to see grey seal pups with their fluffy white coats and try to spot more elusive harbour seal pups.

A FAMILY AFFAIR?

The 'wow' factor associated with many natural spectacles provides a great way to help enthuse children about nature and science. While some activities are perhaps too risky, many can be done as part of a family day or night out. Examples include fairly predictable events, such as the annual appearance of bluebells, or big adventures, such as visiting a tidal island. Staying up late to see meteors or a supermoon are other possibilities.

Spectacles with the lowest scores in the grading system provide a good start and researching when and where to go can be part of the fun. Of course, before a visit you need to take extra care to check any safety precautions highlighted in this guide and for your destination. Having a backup plan is usually a good idea too in case there are no sightings on the day.

ABOVE Watching a lunar eclipse might be a family activity. This image shows the progression of a total eclipse viewed from northwest England in September 2015.

ABOVE Autumn colours in the Scottish Highlands.

A SPECTACULAR YEAR

One of the joys of natural spectacles is that you can follow your interests, choosing when and where to go. However, planning ahead definitely helps your chances of a sighting. So, what would a year look like if you tried to see as much as possible?

As a start, soon after New Year you might try to see the blue and yellow-white streaks of the Quadrantids meteor shower. Winter is also a good time to spot the Northern Lights so keep an eye on alerting services and be ready for a quick departure when conditions look promising.

By mid-January, the first snowdrops should be appearing in southern England, and will soon be getting into full flow further north – look out for snowdrop festivals in your area. Days are now starting to get longer and in March some of the highest tides of the year occur, great for spotting tidal bores and tidal races.

As spring gets underway, bluebells and cherry blossoms appear, but be quick to catch them at their best. Seabirds also start returning to our shores, nesting on vertiginous ledges around the coast, while wading birds form huge flocks over estuaries and wetlands. April showers may trigger spectacular thunderstorms, while high pressure over the North Sea can bring Britain's only named wind, the Helm.

The warm days of summer are a great time for exploring, perhaps making a low tide walk to a tidal island or visiting a seabird city. With luck you might even spot a newly born harbour seal pup. Although the Northern Lights are no longer visible, mysterious noctilucent clouds occasionally dazzle with their electric-blue colours. This is also a prime season for supermoons. In August, the Perseids meteor shower is perhaps one of the most relaxing to watch if you catch a warm, clear night.

As autumn approaches, the annual deer rut begins, which is most magical if you make an early start or stay out until dusk. Trees start to glow with yellows, browns and oranges and the tides are again high enough to cause some spectacular tidal bores and tidal races. Salmon also begin their annual journey to mountain streams, leaping weirs and waterfalls as they go, and migratory geese return, appearing in their thousands at dawn and dusk.

The colder days of winter then give the chance to see other treats, including frozen waterfalls and grey seal pups with their fluffy white coats. You also get a second chance to spot the Northern Lights.

There are also phenomena that can occur at any time of year, such as spraybows and mountain waves. However, you may have to wait longer to see a sunken village reappear or a lunar or solar eclipse.

After watching spectacles for a while, you may find yourself becoming more in tune with the natural rhythm of the tides, seasons and moon, developing a better feel for where and when to go. Many people use social media and/or apps to help to improve the chances of a sighting. You might even find yourself avidly checking the space weather forecast each morning to see if there is any chance of seeing the Northern Lights!

VISITING NATURAL SPECTACLES

While some sights such as autumn leaves may be just a short walk away, others require some travel and perhaps a cliffside walk or rocky scramble. Appropriate clothing and footwear is essential, especially in cold or wet weather and at night. If in doubt, check the websites of organisations such as the Ramblers for advice on outdoor wear and skills and/or visit a specialist outdoor shop. Check destination websites too in case opening hours are seasonal.

Most sights can be seen without any outside help, but some must only be tackled with a guide – low tide walks across Morecambe Bay are one example. However, your chances of a sighting often improve if you go with an expert or fellow enthusiasts. Watch out for walks and workshops in your local area, for example red deer safaris, live viewings of eclipses, guided walks along bluebell trails and birdwatching trips. Good places to look include the websites of the National Trust, RSPB, Wildfowl & Wetlands Trust, Wildlife Trusts, and local wildlife, nature or astronomy groups. You might also find privately operated guided safaris and photography tours, particularly to more remote areas. Although not covered in this guide, these various ideas may improve the chances of a sighting and the enjoyment of a day out too.

BELOW Boat trips are the only way to reach some sites and can be great fun, often with an expert commentary included. Most operators use motor launches or high speed Rigid Hull Inflatable Boats (RHIBs).

	Natural spectacle	Jan	Feb	Mar	Apr	May	Jun	Jul	Aug	Sep	Oct	Nov	Dec
SPACE	Meteor showers	Perseids, Geminids												
	Eclipses and supermoons	Eclipses												
		Supermoons												
	Northern Lights	Aurora borealis												
		Noctilucent clouds												
WEATHER	Hidden currents	Thunderstorms												
		Inversions/valley fog												
	Mountain clouds	Lenticular clouds												
		Cap and banner clouds												
	Named winds and weather	Helm Cloud and Bar												
		The Haar												
TIDES	Tidal bores	Severn Bore												
	Tidal races	Falls of Lora												
	Low tide walks	Holy Island												

	1	2	3	4	5	6	7	8	9	10	11	12
LAND												
Autumn colours	V			M								V
Wildflower displays — Snowdrops								M	L		L	V
Wildflower displays — Bluebells						L	L					
Wildflower displays — Cherry blossom				L								
Rutting deer — Red/fallow/sika deer	V	V	V	L								
Rutting deer — Roe deer		L										
WATER												
Salmon runs — Scottish rivers		V	V	V	V	V	V	V	V	V		
Sunken villages	V	V	V	V	V	V	V	V	V	V	V	V
Wild waterfalls — Reservoir flows	V	V	V	V	V	V	V	V	V	V	V	V
COAST												
Whirling waterbirds — Wading birds	L	L	L	L				L	L		L	L
Whirling waterbirds — Geese	L	L	L									L
Seabird cities — Gannets, puffins					L	L	L					
Seal pups — Grey seals	L		V	V	V						L	
Seal pups — Common seals						L	L					

KEY

Most likely time of year	
Less likely or intermittent	
Dates vary from year to year	

ABOVE Indicative timings for some of the most popular natural spectacles; see chapters for more examples and details on timings.

TIDAL PREDICTIONS AND SAFETY

To safely enjoy the tidal and coastal spectacles in this book, you need to have a basic understanding of the tides and take notice of any local or online warnings or guidance. In particular, the speed and power of the flow for tidal spectacles can far exceed anything you might be used to from a day at the beach. In some places, water levels may rise several metres in a couple of hours – more than the height of most houses – and currents race along faster than an Olympic swimmer.

The tides are caused by the gravitational pull of the sun and the moon. In most places in the UK they rise and fall twice a day. The highest tides are called spring tides and occur roughly every two weeks, reaching a maximum around the spring and autumn equinoxes, which is roughly when the clocks change to and from British Summer Time. The origin of the term 'spring tide' is lost in the mists of time but is nothing to do with the season. The converse is a neap tide which is when tides are unusually low. The time of high tide typically advances by about 50 minutes per day.

Oceanographers estimate the tides for years ahead using complex computer programs and their predictions are surprisingly accurate. However, storms can cause values to differ on the day so you need to allow a safety margin by not leaving things to the last minute. In any case, going out in high winds or waves is often risky as levels may be much higher than expected and waves can knock you off your feet. Always check weather forecasts and warnings first.

Useful sources of tidal predictions include the 'Coast and Sea' section of the BBC Weather website, and the websites of the Met Office, Admiralty EasyTide and the National Tidal and Sea Level Facility (NTSLF). Apps to use on smartphones are also available. Key items to note are the time of high or low tide and the expected values for the closest location(s) to your destination. Times are usually but not always corrected for summer and winter time – do check if they are in GMT/UTC or local time (BST). If Coordinated Universal Time is used, this is equivalent to Greenwich Mean Time, and written as UTC.

Online tidal predictions are usually given for the next few days, sometimes with values further ahead as a paid service. To help with planning further ahead, it is worth looking out for the small tide table booklets often on sale in local tourist offices, newsagents and lifeboat charity shops in coastal regions. Although only for a small geographic area, they usually give values for a full calendar year. Some are available to purchase online. The excellent *Reeds PBO Small Craft Almanac* provides a UK-wide source of information.

When enjoying a day out at the coast or around an estuary, it is useful to know about tidal cut-off and rip currents. The RNLI website describes some of the main risks, such as water creeping in between you and your path to safety, potentially leaving you stranded as the tide rises. Other potential dangers include quicksand, which can set around your legs like concrete, and fast flowing tidal currents, impossible to swim against. It is therefore important not to venture out onto saltmarshes, mudflats or sandbanks, and to stay above high water levels.

Flooding is a risk on stormy or wet days so check for storm and flood warnings too. Key sources include the Met Office website and those of the Environment Agency, SEPA, Natural Resources Wales or NI Direct. Surfers, kayakers, paddle boarders and sailing enthusiasts face additional challenges, but these are beyond the scope of this book.

COUNTRYSIDE CODE

For many of the spectacles in this guide, it is important to be aware of the Countryside Code so as not to disrupt wildlife or spoil things for local residents or other visitors. The code's main themes are respect for other people, protecting the natural environment, enjoying the outdoors, and knowing the signs and symbols of the countryside. For England and Wales, the full version is on gov. uk, while the Scottish Outdoor Access Code and NI Direct Countryside Code have their own useful advice. If you can, it is also good to support local businesses by visiting local pubs, restaurants and cafés, and using local accommodation.

RIGHT The first page of a leaflet about the Countryside Code available from the UK government website (www.gov.uk). © The Countryside Code

The Countryside Code

Your guide to enjoying parks and waterways, coast and countryside

Respect everyone _____
- be considerate to those living in, working in and enjoying the countryside
- leave gates and property as you find them
- do not block access to gateways or driveways when parking
- be nice, say hello, share the space
- follow local signs and keep to marked paths unless wider access is available

Protect the environment _____
- take your litter home - leave no trace of your visit
- do not light fires and only have BBQs where signs say you can
- always keep dogs under control and in sight
- dog poo - bag it and bin it - any public waste bin will do
- care for nature - do not cause damage or disturbance

Enjoy the outdoors _____
- check your route and local conditions
- plan your adventure - know what to expect and what you can do
- enjoy your visit, have fun, make a memory

www.gov.uk/countryside-code

ABOVE & OPPOSITE TOP High and low tide at the causeway to Cramond Island in Edinburgh, illustrating the high tidal range here. The photographs were taken about 16 hours apart.

BELOW A warning sign at Arnside, a great viewpoint for a tidal bore known as the Arnside Bore. Due to the dangers from the tides, during the main tourist season a warning siren sounds twice before the tide arrives.

EXTREME DANGER
BEWARE
FAST RISING TIDES
QUICKSANDS
HIDDEN CHANNELS
IN AN EMERGENCY DIAL 999 - COASTGUARD
· SIREN WARNS OF INCOMING TIDE

NATURAL SPECTACLES FAR AND NEAR

Sights around the world

One of the challenges but also joys of natural spectacles is that you can always travel further, wait longer or go to more extreme environments to see more. While those listed in this guide are an excellent start, it is worth asking what else you might see in the UK and overseas.

Of the space themes, the meteor showers and eclipses we see in the British Isles are every bit as good as elsewhere, although perhaps with less chance of clear cloud-free nights. While the Northern Lights are often more impressive further north, the thrill of a good sighting here is perhaps greater, as they are more difficult to spot.

Weather spectacles give a good showing too, although thunderstorms rarely spawn tornadoes as they do in the plains of the USA. We even have our own named wind, although the Helm perhaps sounds less romantic than the Mistral of France or Scirocco of the Mediterranean. The sight of peaks rising above an inversion is appreciated by hillwalkers and mountaineers worldwide, including in the high mountains of the British Isles.

On high tides, the UK can claim one of the largest whirlpools in the world and a tidal bore that was the birthplace of tidal bore surfing. Undeniably,

PHOTOGRAPHY TIPS

From leaping salmon to the flashes of meteors, many skills are required to take photographs of natural spectacles. This can be part of the fun of a trip, as long as you don't forget to step back from the camera occasionally and enjoy the view.

Often a smartphone or compact camera will provide a reasonable snapshot for many of the weather and tidal phenomena. However, for more challenging topics, a mirrorless or DSLR camera will often give better results, along with a telephoto or zoom lens for wildlife photography. Where possible, shooting in RAW gives more options when post-processing and is particularly important for photography at night. Some subjects, such as birds in flight or leaping salmon, require fast shutter speeds and some photographers use continuous shooting too. Additional tips are given later in the relevant sections.

Note, with all wildlife photography it is important to remember that the welfare of the animals comes first. Watch out for your own safety, particularly when photographing seals and deer. Good practice guides include the RSPB's Birdwatchers' Code and the Nature Photographers' Code of Practice from the Royal Photographic Society.

Long exposures are required at night, typically with high ISO settings, wide angle lenses, wide apertures and a tripod too. Manual focussing is essential, typically choosing a bright star or distant light as a focal point, while a remote trigger or the camera's self-timer can help to reduce shake. Meteor and moon photography have additional challenges, which are described later.

Interesting or unusual angles can add interest, for example taking close-ups of wildflowers from low down or including a hill, trees or landmark in the foreground when photographing clouds, the Northern Lights, meteors or the moon. Astrophotography guides give many more tips, including how to maintain your night vision, avoid star trails and avoid your camera lenses fogging up.

Of course, this brief introduction only gives a flavour of the techniques used and there are many excellent books and online resources available. Photographic and astronomical societies are another good way to learn new skills, as are mentoring schemes and workshops by expert photographers. Mastering all of these techniques could radically improve your skills as a photographer.

though, there are larger tidal bores, with the Qiantang Tidal Bore or *Silver Dragon* of China topping the list. Low tide walks seem to be a particularly British interest, although other examples can be found from around the world, perhaps most dramatically in the Bay of Fundy in Canada where the tidal range narrowly beats that of the Severn Estuary for the highest in the world.

It is with land-based spectacles that the main differences appear, as we have none of the vast herds seen in other parts of the world, like the annual migrations of a million or more wildebeest in East Africa, and of caribou or reindeer in Canada, Alaska and Scandinavia. However, the Scottish Highlands sometimes see red deer herds about a thousand strong.

We also do not see desert flowers bloom after rain, although the Hebrides and Cornwall have wildflower displays every bit as spectacular, and carpets of bluebells are a particularly British phenomenon. Some country parks and arboretums give a flavour of the vivid autumn colours of Japan and New England, while cherry blossoms can be seen in many places around the UK.

In rivers and reservoirs, although waterfalls and ruined villages may be smaller, and there are no volcanic areas to cause eruptions or geysers as in

BELOW Distant peaks rise from a sea of haze viewed from the volcano Popocatépetl in Mexico.

Iceland or the USA, sightings are every bit as interesting. We might not have hungry bears waiting on riverbanks as they do in western Canada and Alaska, but the annual salmon run is otherwise little different to that in Europe and the USA. Although species differ, coastal bird displays are often as impressive as anywhere else worldwide, as are seal numbers around the coast.

The ones that got away

Many other British spectacles could have been included in this book but were left out because they are more challenging to see or predict, especially if you are just starting out. Tornadoes are one example, which while not as severe as in the USA, do occur in the UK, averaging almost 40 recorded sightings per year according to the Tornado and Storm Research Organisation (TORRO).

Many keen hillwalkers are also likely to have seen unusual optical weather phenomena, such as broken spectres, crepuscular rays or fogbows. These occur due to the interactions between sunlight and the clouds and atmosphere but were too ephemeral to include in this guide. Rarer double

BELOW Wildebeest run across a sandy riverbed of the Sand River as they arrive at Kenya's Masai Mara National Reserve from Tanzania's Serengeti National Park during the start of the annual migration. © Getty/Tony Karumba/AFP

rainbows also fall into this category, as do the occasional episodes of blood rain caused by red dust whipped up by strong winds or storms and carried from the Sahara.

By contrast, some wildlife spectacles were left out because they tend to be more the preserve of wildlife experts and documentary makers. Spotting boxing mountain hares is one example. However, on the boat trips mentioned in this guide, you might be lucky enough to spot dolphins or porpoises, and perhaps even a basking shark.

AN INTERCONNECTED WORLD

The more you watch natural spectacles, the more you realise how many events are connected. The seasons are perhaps the most obvious example, resulting from the orbit of the Earth around the sun, affecting wildflowers, bird migration, the deer rut and autumn leaves.

The moon also plays a key role. The highest tides occur when the gravitational pulls of the sun and moon combine, producing powerful tidal bores and tidal races. Usually this is one or two days after a full moon. Supermoons occur when a full moon is particularly close to the Earth, which happens just a few times a year. Wildlife can be affected too, such as with pink-footed geese staying out to feed by moonlight rather than returning to safety offshore. On a practical level, both the Northern Lights and meteors are more difficult to spot during a full moon.

The weather is another key influence. For example, air temperatures and wind speeds affect bird migration, and a cold spring can delay the onset of bluebells. A fine summer followed by a few dry, cold days in autumn can make leaves dazzle more brightly, unless storms suddenly strip the trees bare. If there is a lot of dust in the atmosphere, the colours of a total lunar eclipse can be very different from when skies are clear. At a more basic level, a cloudy night may put an early end to any stargazing, while weather phenomena such as thunderstorms, inversions and mountain waves only appear under specific meteorological conditions.

Looking to the future, it seems likely that climate change will impact on many of the spectacles described in this guide. In particular, wildlife needs to adjust to changes in the seasons, and reservoir levels may be affected more often during droughts. More extreme flooding seems a likely consequence too.

The interconnections are complex and slight changes in one aspect can have knock-on effects in others. For example, if insects hatch earlier, garden birds may find less food available to bring up their chicks, putting them at risk. In the oceans, warming seas may affect salmon growth and

BELOW Illustration of the drivers, changes and potential impacts due to climate change. © Met Office; Contains public sector information licensed under the Open Government Licence v3.0

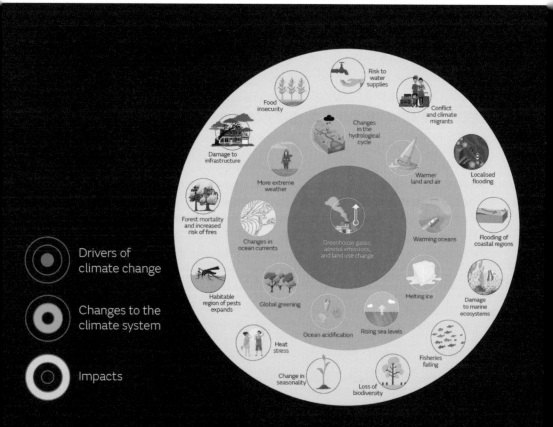

the seal breeding season and cause key prey to move north, such as the sand eels favoured by puffins and seals. Timing mismatches of this type are a key concern throughout the food chain, and are an aspect of the science of phenology, which concerns the timing of recurrent natural events, such as the migration of birds and first flowering of plants.

NATURE'S CALENDAR

One research project tracking these changes is Nature's Calendar, which is run by the Woodland Trust in collaboration with the UK Centre for Ecology and Hydrology. For more than 20 years the project has been collecting a wealth of evidence on the timing of natural events for a range of flowers, shrubs, trees, birds and amphibians. Examples include the dates of the first lawn cuts of the year, the first bluebells appearing and the first nest building by garden birds. Records have been contributed by thousands of volunteers around the UK.

Seasonal reports are published each year and the records are added to a database that stretches back almost 300 years, including findings from the pioneering research of Robert Marsham and Gilbert White in the 18th century. This is used by researchers worldwide to study how the timing of events changes with climate, for example, showing that snowdrops now tend to flower earlier than a few decades ago. Phenological studies such as these are increasingly important in understanding the impacts of climate change.

The Nature's Calendar team invites new volunteers to join them with the following request:

Help us track the effects of weather and climate change on wildlife near you. What effect has recent weather had on wildlife? Does climate change affect timings in nature? Join Nature's Calendar and help scientists discover answers to these questions. From leaf buds bursting to blackberries ripening, let us know what's happening near you. You'll be contributing to a long biological record that dates back as far as 1736.

Observations are recorded via the project website and volunteers include dog walkers, families and gardeners (naturescalendar. woodlandtrust.org.uk).

Observatories and International Dark Sky Association places

North Ronaldsay

Glenlivet &Tomintoul

Coll

Moffat

Northumberland National Park
Kielder Water & Forest Park

Galloway Forest Park

OM Dark Sky Park
& Observatory

North York Moors
National Park

Yorkshire National Park

Snowdonia National Park

Bardsey Island

Elan Valley Estate

Bannau Brycheiniog
National Park

Royal Observatory
Greenwich

Exmoor National Park

Cranborne
Chase

Moore's Reserve
(South Downs National Park)

Bodmin Moor

West Penwith

Sark

SPACE

CHAPTER 1

METEOR SHOWERS

Watch bright flashes of light as a meteor passes through the atmosphere.
Try to spot a fireball on a crisp, winter evening.

Highlights

◆	◆	◆
Watch a meteor shower on a warm summer night	Look out for fireballs streaking across the sky	See meteors fall like rain in a rare meteor storm

What you might see

Meteors or shooting stars occur when particles of space dust and rock burn up in the atmosphere, leaving bright trails behind. The best chances of a sighting are when the Earth passes through the orbital debris left by a comet or asteroid, causing a meteor shower. Several bright showers occur each year, with exotic names such as the Geminids, Leonids, Orionids, Perseids and Quadrantids. With luck you may even spot a fireball brighter than any planet passing through the sky.

Level of difficulty

LOCATION requires dark skies for the best chance of a sighting

FREQUENCY several bright showers occur each year but meteor numbers vary

PREDICTABILITY dates are easy to predict but clouds and moonlight affect sightings

SAFETY normal outdoor risks, with care needed in dark, cold and/or remote locations

Level ★★★ for the Perseids and Geminids, Level ★★★★ to ★★★★★ for fireballs and other popular meteor showers, Level ★★★★★+ for meteor storms

OPPOSITE A Perseid meteor flashes across the night sky above Corfe Castle in Dorset on 12 August 2016. © Getty/Dan Kitwood/Staff

PREVIOUS PAGES Aurora borealis on the Isle of Lewis on 8 October 2013. © Getty/Colin Cameron - Photography

NATURE'S FIREWORKS

Shooting stars or meteors are one of the great sights of the night sky and occur when particles of space dust or rock burn up in the atmosphere. Most are destroyed in transit, but a few reach the ground as meteorites. Typically, they appear at heights of about 80–120km (50–75 miles) above the Earth's surface, close to the outer reaches of the atmosphere.

With clear skies and a lot of patience, you can see meteors on most nights and several normally occur each hour, known as sporadic meteors. However, chances improve greatly during a meteor shower, sometimes with sightings of more than 100 per hour. Meteor showers usually happen when the Earth passes through the debris left by a comet, although a few are caused by fragments of dust and rock from asteroids.

Dozens of meteor showers occur each year, but only a few are bright enough to see with the naked eye. Some of the most popular and prolific are the Perseids in August, the Orionids in October and the Leonids, Geminids and Quadrantids in November, December and January respectively. Events

BELOW NASA photographer Bill Ingalls captured this photograph of a meteor zipping across the night sky on 11 August 2021 during the peak of the Perseid shower. Ingalls shot the 30-second exposure from the summit of Spruce Mountain in West Virginia. A few thin clouds lingered, reflecting light from distant urban areas. © NASA's Earth Observatory

usually build up to a peak over several days or weeks before falling away again. The chances of a sighting are normally best around the peak but of course decrease if there is a lot of cloud or a full moon.

Predictions are published widely online, and good places to look are the Royal Observatory Greenwich and Time and Date websites. Typically, these list a range of dates when sightings are possible, the night of the peak and the expected number per hour at the peak. Sometimes they include the colours expected to appear, along with how fast-moving and persistent trails are likely to be.

Stargazing guides and almanacs are another good source of information and often include predictions for other interesting astronomical events, such as eclipses and planetary alignments.

Sometimes so many meteors appear that a shower is designated as a meteor storm, with the usual criterion being that more than 1,000 meteors should appear per hour. The Leonid meteor storm of 1833 is perhaps the most famous, reportedly briefly reaching 100,000 per hour. NASA maintains a fascinating webpage of eyewitness memories from a later (1966) Leonid storm, in which observers described the sky as being full of meteors, appearing like a blizzard or snowstorm at times.

WATCHING METEOR SHOWERS

Picking your time

For the best chances of seeing a meteor shower, you need dark skies away from the lights of towns and cities. Coastal areas, upland reservoirs and open farmland are popular viewing destinations. To reduce interference from moonlight, it is often best to go out before the moon rises, after it sets or around the time of a new moon. Most websites and guides that list meteor showers include the phases of the moon. Also, smartphones and stargazing apps can help with information on sunset and sunrise times, phases of the moon and the locations of constellations.

The sky should be clear so check television or web-based forecasts before heading out – the Met Office's UK Weather Map has useful cloud cover forecasts. Satellite images are also useful and freely available on most meteorological forecast websites. It is often worth comparing forecasts from several sources to build up a picture of what is likely to happen.

If cloud is forecast or moonlight might spoil the view, sometimes it is still worth going out on a night shortly before or after the peak. This gives the chance of a sighting, although you may have to wait longer before success as hourly rates will be less.

Finding the radiant

Meteor showers usually seem to originate from a small patch of sky known as the radiant and are named after the constellation or brightest star closest to this point. Thus, the Perseids are named after the constellation Perseus and the Orionids after one of the best-known constellations of all: the hunter Orion, of Greek mythology. In reality, of course, this is an optical illusion since meteors appear at the outer edges of the atmosphere rather than in deep space.

When particles hit the atmosphere, they are travelling in much the same direction, but due to perspective, meteors seem longer to the side of the radiant. This is similar to the way that motorway or railway tracks appear to converge to a point when looking into the distance. For that reason, the usual advice is to look to the side of the radiant rather than directly at it. The best viewing times are often said to be from midnight to dawn, when the radiant is at its highest, but you may still spot meteors earlier in the night when it is closer to the horizon.

When you look up the dates of a meteor shower, you will usually find information on the location of the radiant and how it will vary during the night. Sometimes this is a description, such as *'look high in the sky to the northeast from about midnight'*, while other sources are more technical, giving the predicted azimuth or direction and altitude for each hour. Some even show a graphical representation of where to look and the nearest constellations. The azimuth is similar to a compass bearing but expressed relative to true

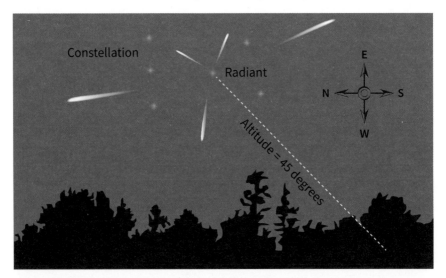

ABOVE Illustration of the radiant and the constellation after which the meteor shower is named. In this hypothetical example the radiant is due east of the observer and at an altitude of about 45 degrees to the horizon. © NASA's Earth Observatory

north, while the altitude is the angle relative to the horizon. For example, if both azimuth and altitude were 45 degrees the radiant would be on roughly a northeasterly compass bearing about halfway between the horizon and vertically overhead.

For beginners, this can all seem very technical. Just dive in at the level at which you feel most comfortable, and once you've seen a meteor you will probably want to learn more.

Watching and waiting

Having found a suitably dark place, it is then a case of lying back and waiting, slowly scanning the skies for those elusive flashes of light. Groups and families have an advantage as they can watch different areas and shout if they spot anything: 'wow' and 'hey' will do if lost for words. Typically it takes at least 15–30 minutes for your eyes to adjust to the night so avoid looking at any source of light, such as phone or camera screens or car headlights.

Even in summer, nights can be cold, particularly if there is any wind, so it is best to wrap up warm and take more clothing than you think you will need. That may include gloves, a hat, waterproofs, snacks, a hot drink and a sleeping bag or blanket. A torch is also essential. Experts often take a fold-up chair or mat to make life easier, and use red filters and settings on torches and smartphones to reduce the effects of dazzle on their night vision.

The number of meteors you see will depend on your experience and eyesight, and even experts rarely see the rates quoted for the peak. Indeed, to allow comparisons between meteor showers, peak rates are often for a theoretical quantity called the Zenithal Hourly Rate, which is the number that would occur if the radiant was directly overhead in a near perfect dark sky. Values vary from year to year, depending on where a comet or asteroid is in its journey through space and hence the density of orbital dust it has left in its path.

Staying safe in the dark

When viewing meteor showers, just getting to a viewpoint is sometimes an adventure, with strange noises in the distance and mysterious silhouettes appearing in the dark.

In all the excitement it is important not to forget your safety so, if possible, check out new viewpoints in daylight first. Even then it can be difficult to orientate yourself unless you know the constellations; a compass or a smartphone compass app helps.

As well as being more fun, meteor watching with others is safer as you never know who else will be around in the dark. However, try to avoid disturbing local residents with excessive noise. In winter, snow and ice are

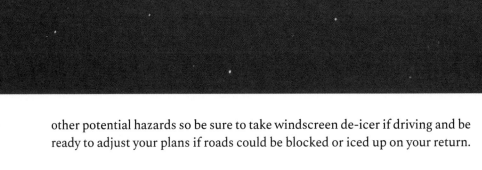

other potential hazards so be sure to take windscreen de-icer if driving and be ready to adjust your plans if roads could be blocked or iced up on your return.

DIRTY SNOWBALLS

Comets are often described as 'dirty snowballs' due to their mix of ice and debris. The nucleus is typically up to a few miles across and is made up of dust, water ice and frozen gases such as ammonia, carbon dioxide and methane. Most have elliptical orbits that take them far out into space, only returning to the solar system every few decades or more. Perhaps the most famous is Comet Halley – often called Halley's Comet – which was last visible to the eye in 1986 and is due to return in 2061.

The classical long, drawn-out tail seen in many images normally results from melting and evaporation during a comet's slingshot passage past the sun. The solar wind causes minute particles to spread out alongside the orbital path and over thousands of years it is these that cause meteor showers rather than the visible tail. Usually the Earth only passes through a comet's

WHICH METEOR SHOWERS TO WATCH?

With ten or more significant meteor showers occurring each year, it can be difficult to know which to choose for a night's viewing. Mark Phillips, President of the Astronomical Society of Edinburgh, has seen many. If you are just starting out he suggests:

Two of the best and most reliable meteor showers of the year are the Perseids in August and the Geminids in December. Watching the Perseids is definitely more comfortable in those warm summer nights with the Milky Way high overhead, and they sometimes produce some of the best rates of up to 150 meteors per hour at their peak, including quite a few bright fireballs.

Wrap up warm for the Geminids and you won't be disappointed. The skies are darker in winter with the impressive constellation of Orion dominating the sky and they'll still peak at around 100 meteors per hour under ideal conditions. The Geminids are interesting as they come from the asteroid Phaethon (most showers come from comets) and they can appear to be different colours due to metals such as calcium and sodium. The meteors are also relatively slow compared to other showers so they appear to last a little longer.

With any shower a bright moon can hide many of the fainter meteors so a shower close to new moon will always be better. The best rates will be visible when the radiant is at its highest above your horizon and peak rates are based on the radiant being at the zenith.

The Leonids in November are a little different as every 33 years or so they have been known to deliver a real meteor storm with rates of over 1,000 meteors per hour. The next such storm may be in 2034, fingers crossed.

You don't need anything other than a little patience to observe meteors. Just lie back in a reclining chair if you can (saves a lot of neck pain) and look up. The advice is usually to look about 30–40 degrees away from the radiant and about 60 degrees up to get a good chance of seeing more meteors. But remember, meteors can appear in any part of the sky at any time. The closer to the radiant they are, the shorter the trails will be – further away, trails appear longer.

ABOVE Even in a city, it is sometimes possible to photograph meteors as in this example, taken at the coast in Edinburgh in the pool of darkness beside a building near the peak of a Geminids meteor shower.

orbital path once per year, causing a single meteor shower. However, it meets that of Comet Halley twice, causing the Eta Aquarids in May and the Orionids in October.

METEOROIDS AND METEORITES

The particles left behind by a comet or asteroid are often smaller than a grain of sand and are known as meteoroids – the name given to any small particles found in space. Typically, they are separated by many miles, so even in a 'dense' layer they are still a long way apart.

Speeds on first hitting the atmosphere can exceed 240,000km/h (150,000mph), generating very high temperatures as the air is compressed ahead of their path. This is enough to vaporise smaller particles, energising nearby atmospheric molecules and leaving a light-emitting trail of plasma in the meteor's wake.

Meteor showers often have characteristic combinations of colours, which experts use in addition to the direction of travel to distinguish them from the occasional sporadic meteors seen on most nights. For example, greens indicate a high nickel content and purples a high calcium content.

Speed can have an effect too. If the brightness exceeds a certain visual magnitude roughly similar to that of Venus they are called fireballs. These are often visible over whole regions and sometimes explode due to the thermal stresses caused, at which point they are known as bollides.

While most particles burn up in the atmosphere, some make it to the ground as meteorites. These are usually the remains of debris from asteroids, usually with their surfaces melted and scarred from their passage through the atmosphere. Most date back to the origins of the solar system about 4.6 billion years ago, providing scientists with insights into how the planets were formed. They might therefore be regarded as a

RIGHT Astronauts from the International Space Station captured this unusual view of a Perseid meteor descending into the Earth's atmosphere in August 2011.
© NASA's Earth Observatory

type of space delivery service, bringing much larger samples to Earth than it is possible to collect on a space mission. The disadvantages, of course, are the damage and contamination caused by their journey through the atmosphere and the highly unpredictable nature of their arrival.

Following the sighting of a massive fireball, the Winchcombe Meteorite of 2021 was the first to be recovered in the UK for 30 years. More than half a kilogram of material was collected and samples are on display at Winchcombe Museum and the Natural History Museum in London. The Winchcombe Meteorite website has an entertaining account of the event and subsequent findings, which made both local and national news.

Some meteorites are large enough to leave craters and one of the best examples is Meteor Crater in Arizona, also known as the Barringer Crater. It is more than a kilometre across and is thought to have been caused by

the impact of an iron meteorite about 50,000 years ago. The largest fragment recovered – the Holsinger Meteorite – is almost a metre across and on display at the nearby Discovery Center & Space Museum. The main meteorite may have been almost 50m (164ft) in diameter.

DARK SKY SITES

When looking for meteors, if skies are clear perhaps the single best way to improve your chances is to find an area well away from artificial light. Even if no meteors appear, it can still be staggering to see so many stars if you are only used to a town or city night. Sometimes this includes the Milky Way in all its glory, much as it would have looked in prehistoric times.

To give more people the chance to experience this, several dark sky sites have been established around the UK in recent years. The International Dark-Sky Association (IDA) designates these as urban night sky places, or dark sky parks, communities, reserves or sanctuaries. For example, a dark sky park is defined as 'land possessing an exceptional or distinguished quality of starry nights and a nocturnal environment that is specifically protected for its scientific, natural, educational, cultural heritage, and/or public enjoyment.'

The map at the start of this section shows the locations of dark sky sites in the British Isles. Some of the larger sites have observatories equipped with telescopes and an active programme of workshops, talks and stargazing sessions. Some groups organise dark sky festivals each year.

OPPOSITE Aerial view of Barringer Crater (meteor impact) in Arizona. © Getty/StephanHoerold

ABOVE Kielder Observatory in Northumberland is at the heart of one of the largest dark sky parks in Europe and runs events throughout the year on astronomy, auroras, astrophotography, meteors and stargazing. © Kielder Observatory

If the nearest dark sky site is too far away, light pollution maps give clues on where to visit. These are typically based on satellite and/or ground-based observations over a period of time. Links to several appear on the IDA's website and more can be found by searching online. To use them, simply find your location and look for the darkest places nearby that would be safe and easy to reach on your next astronomical adventure.

Other ways to learn more about stargazing include joining one of the many amateur astronomy groups around the UK, and organisations such as the British Astronomical Association and the Royal Astronomical Society. Your local observatory may also run events open to the public, and observatories can be found in a surprisingly large number of towns and cities. Groups specifically for meteor enthusiasts include the UK Meteor Network, the NEMETODE network and the International Meteor Organization.

PHOTOGRAPHING METEOR SHOWERS

To photograph meteors, many enthusiasts use a DSLR or mirrorless camera, but this requires some specialist techniques if you are only used to daytime photography. Some tips from Mark Phillips include:

To image meteors a camera on a fixed tripod is sufficient, preferably with a remote shutter release, but this is not essential as you can use the camera's delay timer. The length of exposure you can use without stars appearing to trail is dependent on the focal length of the lens you are using. A basic rule of thumb is to divide 500 by the focal length of the lens, and that gives you the exposure in seconds. For example, a 28mm focal length lens should be able to do 18 seconds without any significant trails showing. Work out what the best ISO is for your camera to make it as sensitive as possible without introducing too much noise. Something between 800 and 3,200 should be fine.

Because stars are faint and small your auto-focus may not work well – or at all – so you will probably have to focus the camera manually. This is critical! There's no point spending an evening taking hundreds of exposures only to find that all of them are blurred afterwards. Take some time over this to get it spot on.

Part of the post-processing challenge is then to sift through the images to find good shots of meteors. This includes ruling out satellite trails, which typically appear across several images in a row, whereas the brief flash of a meteor will normally only be on one. With luck you might spot more than one meteor on an image, but this is rare unless you are fortunate enough to catch a meteor storm.

Astronomy enthusiasts often go a stage further and use purpose-made cameras for detecting meteors. Typically, these run from dusk to dawn and are adapted from security cameras or hand-built from sensors, lenses and housings. Using specialist software, they often link automatically to meteor camera networks such as the UK Meteor Network. These volunteer-run networks provide valuable data on meteor astronomy with links to the UK Fireball Alliance, which is led by staff from the Natural History Museum and aims to recover freshly fallen meteorites in the UK.

RIGHT While stargazing, there is always a chance you may see sporadic meteors, as in this photograph taken while watching the Northern Lights on a clear Scottish night.

CHAPTER 2

ECLIPSES AND SUPERMOONS

Watch the shadow of the Earth cross the moon causing a lunar eclipse.
See supermoons in summer, and try to spot a rare partial solar eclipse.

Highlights

◆
See the moon
glow red during a
total lunar eclipse

◆
Watch a supermoon
tower above the
horizon

◆
Spot the moon's
shadow cut across
the sun

What you might see

The moon is one of the most beautiful objects in the night sky, especially when a supermoon occurs. During a total lunar eclipse, it becomes even more special as the shadow of the Earth passes across its face, turning it a beautiful copper-red.

On rare occasions, the moon blocks out the sun during a total solar eclipse, turning day into night, although partial eclipses are more common. As totality approaches, enthusiasts use terms such as a string of beads and diamond ring to describe the amazing sights that appear, followed by the sun's fiery corona.

Level of difficulty ★★★★

LOCATION very location dependent for solar eclipses
FREQUENCY supermoons occur annually, but eclipses are rarer
PREDICTABILITY predictions are remarkably precise but sightings are weather dependent
SAFETY normal outdoor risks at night, with risks to eyesight in solar eclipses

....

Level ★★ for supermoons, Level ★★★★ for lunar eclipses,
Level ★★★★★ for solar eclipses

OPPOSITE A supermoon sets over the Pentland Hills in Scotland shortly before dawn.

CELESTIAL DANCE

Viewed from space, the Earth and moon perform a remarkable dance as night turns to day and a new moon becomes full. Tethered by gravity, the moon orbits the spinning Earth roughly once a month and together they pass around the sun once a year.

The astronomical spectacles caused by this complex motion include full moons, supermoons and lunar and solar eclipses. Full moons occur every month or so and are dubbed supermoons when the moon approaches unusually close to the Earth and appears larger and brighter than usual. Lunar eclipses are rarer and are caused by the shadow of the Earth passing across the face of the moon. In a solar eclipse it is the moon's shadow that seems to take a bite out of the sun.

Total eclipses are the most dramatic, causing the moon to turn coppery red as it is lit only by sunlight filtered through the Earth's atmosphere. Meanwhile, in a solar eclipse the sun's upper atmosphere – the corona – is revealed in all its beauty.

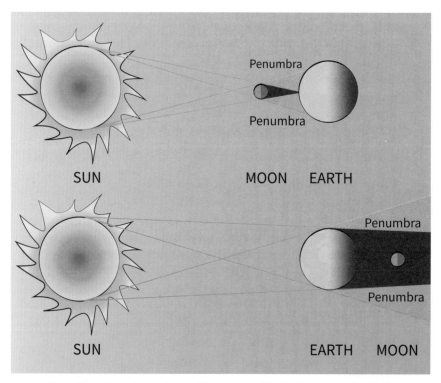

ABOVE Illustration of how the shadows of the moon and the Earth cause a solar (top) and lunar (lower) eclipse. If drawn to scale with the sun a centimetre in diameter, the Earth would be a small dot and more than a metre away.

ABOVE A partial lunar eclipse appears over the London skyline on 16 July 2019.
© Getty/Peter Summers/Stringer

LUNAR ECLIPSES

For most of the time, the moon changes appearance gradually, taking just over 29.5 days to progress from a full moon to a new moon and back again. However, during a lunar eclipse the shadow of the Earth passes across the face of the moon in just a few hours. This only occurs rarely because the orbit of the moon is slightly inclined to that of the Earth around the sun. For an eclipse to occur, the moon therefore needs to pass through the Earth's orbital plane at the same time as the Earth's shadow blocks light reaching it from the sun.

This shadow has two main parts: the outer penumbra where some sunlight still gets through, and a dark inner umbra region. As an eclipse begins, a barely perceptible darkening occurs as the moon enters the penumbra, as if a dimmer switch had been turned down slightly on a lamp. The rounded silhouette of the Earth then appears to eat into the moon's face as it passes through the umbra, causing a partial eclipse.

This becomes a total eclipse if the umbra totally envelopes the moon, and can last for an hour or more. During this time, the moon's surface is lit only by sunlight refracted through the Earth's atmosphere. The light that gets through consists mainly of longer wavelengths, such as reds and oranges,

2. ECLIPSES AND SUPERMOONS

49

whereas greens and blues are scattered more. The result is a beautiful red or brownish reflected glow, often referred to as a blood moon. As with sunsets, the shades vary depending on the amount of dust and clouds in the atmosphere.

On average, total lunar eclipses occur somewhere in the world in most years. Sightings are inevitably less frequent at a given place but, weather permitting, you might hope to see a partial eclipse in most years and a total eclipse at least every few years. Penumbral eclipses are slightly more frequent but less interesting as they are barely perceptible to the eye. The introduction to this book includes another sequence of images of a lunar eclipse.

SUPERMOONS

As the moon travels around the Earth, its distance varies because its orbit is elliptical rather than circular. At its closest, a full moon can seem larger and brighter than usual, making an already beautiful sight even better. This is called a supermoon and several occur each year, usually in consecutive months.

In news reports, full moons and supermoons are often given a name, such as a 'Strawberry Supermoon'. These names date back to ancient times and were often linked to the weather, plants or animals typical for that time of year. In Western cultures, some common names are Wolf, Snow and Worm Moon from January to March, then Egg or Pink, Flower and Strawberry Moon from April to June. These are followed by the Hay or Buck, Grain or Sturgeon and Corn or Harvest Moons from July to September and the Hunter's, Beaver and Cold Moons to end the year. The Harvest Moon is perhaps the best known, with its name possibly linked to it being bright enough to allow farmers to carry on bringing in the harvest after sunset.

While there is usually only one full moon per month, in some years two occur due to the different lengths of the lunar and calendar months. This can

BELOW A sequence of images of the lunar eclipse of 21 January 2019 taken from Edinburgh using a reflecting telescope over slightly more than two hours. From top left they are at the pre-eclipse, penumbra, deeper penumbra, umbra, deeper umbra (x3), total eclipse, deeper eclipse and past eclipse mid-point stages. The images were taken as part of a live streaming event run by the Astronomical Society of Edinburgh and posted online soon after. © Mark Phillips, Astronomical Society of Edinburgh

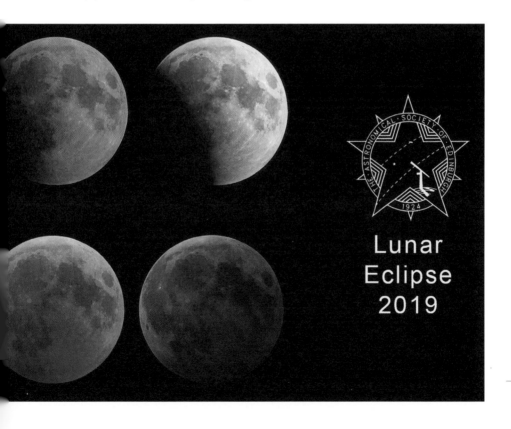

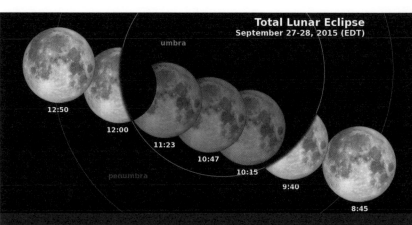

Total Lunar Eclipse
September 27-28, 2015 (EDT)

umbra

12:50

12:00

11:23

10:47

10:15

9:40

8:45

penumbra

ABOVE Diagram showing the moon at various stages of the eclipse with times in Eastern Daylight Time (EDT). © NASA's Scientific Visualization Studio

WATCHING ECLIPSES AND SUPERMOONS

In contrast to many other natural phenomena, the dates and times of eclipses and supermoons can be predicted with extraordinary precision many years ahead. The calculations aren't simple, as factors to consider include the elliptical orbits of the Earth and moon, the non-spherical shape (oblateness) of the Earth, the inclined orbit of the moon, and the influences of other planets in the solar system.

The resulting estimates appear widely on astronomical blogs and websites, for example Royal Museum Greenwich's 'Night Sky Highlights', *BBC Sky at Night Magazine*'s 'Advice' section, the British Astronomical Association's 'Sky Notes' and the Astronomical Society of Edinburgh's 'Sky Diary'. The Time and Date website is another great resource, as are astronomical almanacs and guides (see Further reading). Local and national newspapers often run eclipse and supermoon stories in the run-up to an event.

To improve your chances of a sighting, why not make a plan for the year ahead and weave the relevant dates into your schedule? Two things to watch out for are whether times are in GMT or British Summer Time, and whether the predictions are for your location, as timings vary around the world. For lunar eclipses, the chapter on meteor showers gives essential tips that are also useful for moon watching, such as on predicting cloud cover, keeping warm at night and looking after your personal safety (see pages 35–38). By contrast, for solar eclipses the top priority is to avoid risking your eyesight, as described on pages 56–57.

lead to four full moons in a season, so traditionally the third of these is known as a blue moon to get the naming back on track. This may be the origin of the phrase 'once in a blue moon'.

Perhaps this is going a step too far, but names are sometimes combined further; for example, a 'super blue blood moon' would be a total eclipse of the third full moon in a season when the moon is at or near its closest point to the Earth. A more recent definition for a blue moon is that this is the second full moon in a month, if two occur in the same month.

When watching a supermoon, perhaps the most popular view is as it rises above the horizon, often with a beautiful golden glow from the setting sun. An optical illusion called the 'Moon Illusion' also makes the moon look larger when it is close to the horizon. Enthusiasts use maps, compasses or stargazing apps to find just the right spot to wait for the moon to appear, and it is sometimes worth going out shortly before dawn to see moonset too.

For photographers, a classic image is of the rising lunar disk with an interesting silhouette in the foreground, typically of an ancient monument, tree, mountain peak or famous building. Although slow moving, it can be remarkably difficult to get sharp photographs, and experts often use a tripod, remote shutter release and fast shutter speeds to minimise shake and visual

BELOW A sturgeon supermoon rising behind central Edinburgh.

distortions due to atmospheric turbulence. A zoom or telephoto lens is essential to capture the detail of the moon's surface.

The number of supermoons per year depends on the definition used; three to five is typical. If you look online or in stargazing guides, you will probably find disagreements over the approach to use. Some organisations use a distance-based approach, saying that a supermoon occurs when the moon is within a specific distance of the Earth, while others consider how close it is in percentage terms, based on the difference between the moon's closest and further distances from the Earth.

Astronomers therefore sometimes prefer the name 'Perigee Full Moon' where the moon's perigee is the point on its orbit that is closest to the Earth. Here, the moon appears about 14% larger and 30% brighter than when it is at apogee, its further distance from the Earth. However, for the interested amateur this doesn't matter hugely as both a supermoon and full moon are fascinating to watch.

BELOW The great North American total eclipse of 2017. This is the moment when totality comes to an end and the famous diamond ring is visible. The sun's corona is also still visible, with the star Regulus (the brightest star in the constellation of Leo and one of the brightest stars in the night sky) lying approximately 79 light years from the sun, just to the left of the eclipse. © Getty/John Finney Photography

SOLAR ECLIPSES

Compared with a lunar eclipse, the solar version is a more fiery affair. In a partial eclipse, the moon's shadow seems to take a bite out of the sun, whereas in a total eclipse darkness descends and the sun's corona appears.

For observers, one challenge is that the moon only casts a narrow shadow as its diameter is only about a quarter that of the Earth. Even at its closest (perigee), its umbra is less than a hundred miles wide at the equator and still only a few hundred miles wide at the poles. At ground level, one way to imagine the effect is as a spotlight passing across a stage projecting a shadow rather than light.

To see a solar eclipse, you therefore need to pick your observing location and time carefully. Get it right and those lucky enough to have seen it say the display is truly spectacular, starting with a dark, rounded patch cutting into the disk of the sun. Then, as totality approaches, dramatic short-lived bursts of light appear. Sometimes these are described as a string of beads, also called 'Baily's beads' after the English astronomer Francis Baily, who first coined the phrase in the 19th century.

Baily's beads occur as the sun shines past mountains and valleys on the edge of the moon. The 'diamond ring' effect is the brightest of all, when a single burst shines out in the instant before totality. For a few magical moments the sun then appears as a black disk surrounded by the gentle white light of the corona. The authors of *Totality: Eclipses of the Sun* (see Further reading) describe this moment beautifully:

> *Where the sun once stood, there is a black disk in the sky, outlined by the soft pearly white glow of the corona, about the brightness of a full moon. Small but vibrant reddish features stand at the eastern rim of the moon's disk, contrasting vividly with the white of the corona and the black where the sun is hidden. These are the prominences, giant clouds of hot gas in the sun's lower atmosphere. They are always a surprise, each unique in shape and size, different yesterday and tomorrow from what they are at this special moment.*
> *You are standing in the shadow of the moon.*

Scientists plan experiments around totality to study the sun's upper atmosphere in much more detail than is possible from a satellite. Interestingly, it is a pure quirk of nature that the moon's distance and diameter are just right for this total darkness to occur. However, this won't always be the case, as the moon is slowly drifting away from the Earth. Don't worry though, as the effect won't be noticeable for millions of years.

Total solar eclipses occur somewhere on Earth most years, but to see one you need to be ready and waiting in the so-called Path of Totality, as it rushes towards you at more than 1,000 miles per hour. Typically, they last a few minutes, but sometimes even less if the moon's umbra only just reaches the Earth. Partial eclipses are slightly more frequent – and, of course, presage a total eclipse – as are annular eclipses in which the umbra doesn't quite reach the Earth, causing a so-called 'ring of fire'. Hybrid eclipses also occur, changing from annular to total, then annular again during the shadow's passage.

All this means that, at a given location, you would be lucky to see more than one total solar eclipse in a lifetime. Enthusiasts therefore travel the world to see one, visiting far-flung places and taking trips on cruise ships or chartered aircraft to be in just the right place, at the right time. Often people combine these adventures with local sightseeing.

WATCHING SOLAR ECLIPSES

Most accounts and descriptions of solar eclipses rightly emphasise the danger of viewing the sun directly, because of the risk of blindness or permanent damage to your eyes. Worryingly this may only materialise hours or days later, with no immediate pain. Viewing through binoculars or a telescope is even more foolhardy and sunglasses provide no useful protection. Camera sensors may be damaged too.

A safer way to see a partial or total solar eclipse yourself is to project sunlight on to a piece of white card through a small hole in another piece of card, making a rudimentary pinhole camera. You can find instructions

for refining this approach online: for example, try using an aluminium foil insert to make the hole neater, or experiment with using a kitchen sieve or colander with small holes to project multiple images of the sun on to the card. However, for your safety it is still important to not even glance at the sun while using these approaches.

The best option of all though – and the most practical for many people – is to watch live feeds from news channels and organisations such as Time and Date and the Royal Observatory in Greenwich. Alternatively, you could go to an event organised by a local observatory or astronomy group. Typically these make use of telescopes fitted with special filters with digital feeds to display the image. For example, the BBC held a live broadcast from Cornwall in 1999 for the last total eclipse to be seen in mainland Britain. Sadly, though, the next visible one from the British Isles is many decades away, although partial eclipses are more frequent.

CHAPTER 3

NORTHERN LIGHTS

*See the green arc of the Northern Lights with red
or purple pillars shooting into the sky. Watch mysterious
night-shining clouds during the summer.*

Highlights

♦
See the green arc of
the aurora borealis

♦
Admire the dancing
pillars of the Mirrie
Dancers

♦
Watch mysterious
night-shining clouds

What you might see

From autumn to spring, the Northern Lights sometimes put on a glorious display for a few lucky watchers, glowing green in the night sky. On the best nights, rays and pillars dance skywards, infused with a red and pink glow.

Sightings are most common in Scotland and northern England, but with luck you might even spot them as far south as Cornwall or Kent. As the aurora fade away in summer, wisps of noctilucent clouds sometimes appear, forming electric-blue patterns high in the night sky.

Level of difficulty ★★★★★

LOCATION opportunities improve the further north you go
FREQUENCY the aurora borealis is occasionally visible from autumn to spring
PREDICTABILITY can be forecast to some extent but always unpredictable
SAFETY normal risks of outdoor activities at night

Level ★★★★★ for the Northern Lights (★★★ in northern Scotland),
Level ★★★★ for noctilucent clouds

OPPOSITE Northern Lights viewed from Cley, North Norfolk. © Getty/David Tipling/Universal Images Group

AURORA BOREALIS

The Northern Lights are one of the most awe-inspiring spectacles visible from the British Isles, and near the top of many people's bucket lists. At these latitudes, they typically appear as a green arc across the horizon, sometimes with pink or red rays that push high into the sky. Their Gaelic name of *na fir-chlis* ('nimble dancers') hints at the dancing pillars of light that appear, while the Latin name *aurora borealis* loosely translates as 'dawn of the north'.

For the best chances of a sighting you need to find a dark spot away from artificial lighting with a clear view to the north, ideally on a night with little or no moonlight. Popular viewpoints include north-facing coasts in north Wales, Norfolk, Northern Ireland, Northumberland and the Solway Firth, while in Scotland some of the best displays are seen from the Moray Firth, the Hebrides, Orkney and Shetland. More southerly sightings occur occasionally. North-facing dark sky sites are often good spots too, but that said the brightest displays may be visible above a city's lights, and there are some beautiful photographs online from places such as Edinburgh and Perth.

BELOW Aurora borealis at Scalan in the Braes of Glenlivet in the Tomintoul & Glenlivet – Cairngorms Dark Sky Park. The park was designated in 2018 and is one of the best stargazing sites in Scotland. © Tomintoul & Glenlivet – Cairngorms Dark Sky Park/David Newland of Cairngorms Astronomy Group (CAG)

Auroras occur all year round but are typically drowned out by twilight from May to July. During these months, enthusiasts seek out another spectacle, namely the noctilucent clouds which form graceful blue-silver patterns high in the sky. These reflect light from the sun when it is below the horizon and are visible in the darkest part of the night.

As with any natural phenomena, when looking for them, it is best to travel in hope but be prepared to try again another time if disappointed. For most people, the success rate improves with practice. Rest assured that even some experts are defeated on their first attempts. If skies are clear, the amazing star displays are a compensation, at least.

Why do the Northern Lights occur?

The short answer is that the energy from charged particles from the sun causes atoms and molecules high in the atmosphere around the poles to emit light.

The longer story begins at the sun, which at a distance of 150 million km (93 million miles) has a diameter more than 100 times that of the Earth. Fuelled by nuclear fusion, the sun constantly converts hydrogen to helium, releasing vast amounts of energy and light. This is sufficient to split atoms into ions and electrons, forming a magnetically charged material called plasma, some of which spirals out into the solar system. This so-called solar wind typically passes the Earth after one to three days and interacts with

our own magnetic field – the magnetosphere – causing it to fan out on the opposite side like the tail of a comet.

While many particles stream by, some energise electrons in our own magnetosphere, which follow the magnetic field lines down towards the magnetic poles, causing a continuous background level of auroral activity. This typically occurs in an elliptically shaped ring north of the Arctic Circle known as the auroral oval. The magnetic pole moves over time and in recent years has been located in northern Canada.

Occasionally the solar wind picks up speed, intensifying the display, often due to particles ejected from cooler (less hot) areas on the sun's surface called coronal holes. However, the best displays often occur when the magnetosphere is hit by a burst of additional plasma resulting from a Coronal Mass Ejection (CME). These are often torn off from solar flares associated with sunspots; the website of the USA's National Oceanic and Atmospheric Administration (NOAA) describes these as 'a billion tons of plasma ejected from the sun, traveling at a million miles per hour'.

The strongest auroras usually occur when the magnetic field of the CME is aligned south, providing the energy to accelerate particles in the Earth's magnetosphere into the atmosphere. Remarkably, satellite observations have shown that particles are sometimes catapulted towards the Earth from the tail of the magnetosphere due to a high-energy clash of magnetic field lines called magnetic reconnection. This is another possible factor in intensifying the display.

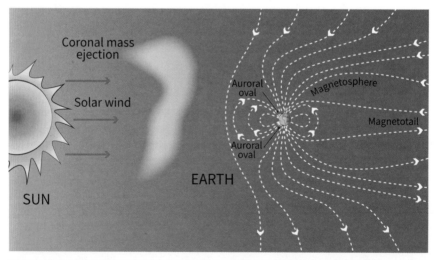

ABOVE Illustration of the solar wind and a Coronal Mass Ejection approaching the magnetosphere. If drawn to scale with the sun a centimetre in diameter, the Earth would be more than a metre away, and the true path of the solar wind would be apparent as it spirals out from the spinning sun.

ABOVE A typical view in the UK for a small to medium event, this one in southeast Scotland, with sightings as far south as South Yorkshire. A green arc of light stretches across the horizon, which in this case was clearly visible by eye.

The reason that we see light is that this extra energy, mainly from electrons, chemically excites atomic oxygen and nitrogen molecules, causing them to emit photons. A neon light works in a similar way. The most common colour is green, which arises from oxygen at lower levels of about 100–150km (62–93 miles) or more, while nitrogen molecules at higher levels mainly emit reds or purples. Oxygen also emits red light at high altitudes and various other colours can appear as others combine. Maximum heights for an aurora are typically 200–300km, but can reach 600km.

All this activity takes some time to build and subside, so displays sometimes occur on two or more consecutive nights. From the side, the auroral oval often appears as a green arc, and this is the classic view from the British Isles. If the oval widens, the arc rises higher in the sky, sometimes with rays or pillars appearing during geomagnetic substorms, which may only last a few minutes. However, a burst of light overhead is much rarer than at higher latitudes.

As the NOAA website notes: 'Given the right vantage point, say for example on top of a hill in the northern hemisphere with an unobstructed view towards the north, a person can see [an] aurora even when it is 1000km further north.'

One intriguing prospect is that sunspot activity roughly follows an 11-year cycle, causing much speculation about whether aurora will be more frequent around future peaks. Solar cycles 25 and 26 are predicted to peak in 2025 and 2036.

This whistlestop tour is, of course, just a brief introduction to the causes of the Northern Lights. The Further reading section has links to books and websites that give much more detailed descriptions of this fascinating phenomenon.

WATCHING THE NORTHERN LIGHTS

For the aurora hunter, many alerting services are available, as described on page 66. However, often only a short warning time is feasible.

If conditions look promising, it is therefore worth being ready to head out at short notice, having already decided on a suitably dark north-facing place to go. Many of the tips described in the chapter on meteor showers apply here too, such as checking the weather, the phase of the moon and cloud cover beforehand to see if it is worth the trip and then, if you do go ahead, taking warm clothing, snacks and drinks. The map on page 30 shows the locations of dark sky sites in the British Isles.

Once at a viewpoint, patience is a virtue as the strength of a display usually varies through the night. Some only last for a few minutes, while others may continue for hours, occasionally forming pillars, rays or curtains stretching higher in the sky. A fully charged smartphone is useful to keep

track of the latest alerts.

When an aurora is predicted, alerting services will sometimes say if it is expected to be visible by eye or, more usually, on camera. Although some people have better colour or night vision than others, a camera usually does better because the sensor picks up light for the whole time that the shutter is open. By contrast, by eye we see more of a snapshot, updated as time moves on, and the rod cells important for night vision give more of a monochrome view, unlike the cone cells we rely on in daylight.

For the serious aurora hunter, it is therefore worth learning the basics of nighttime photography and, as noted in the introduction to this book, wide angle lenses, tripods, remote shutter triggers, high ISO numbers and long exposures are usual (see page 44).

Images can also help settle any doubt about whether the colours you saw really were the Northern Lights rather than the vestiges of a sunset or a city's lights shining on cloud. In addition to reports of sightings, other possible clues include the range of colours, the presence of rays or pillars and whether stars were visible through the lights, indicating a lack of cloud. Having said all that, even a photograph cannot always do full justice to a strong display with its dancing, shimmering lights, leading some enthusiasts to take time-lapse images or videos instead. Smartphones are becoming increasingly more capable of aurora photography.

If your interest and budget stretch to a trip further north, popular destinations include Alaska, Iceland and the northern parts of Canada, Norway, Sweden and Finland. Sightings tend to be much higher in the sky with more shapes and colours, although they are never guaranteed. Other possibilities include charter flights or cruise ship trips specifically to see the Northern Lights and you can find examples online. Even further away, the aurora australis or Southern Lights can best be seen during the British summer, for which popular destinations include the southernmost parts of Australia, New Zealand, Chile and Argentina. For a lucky few, Antarctica provides the best chances of a sighting.

LEFT The Northern Lights above coastal towns in Fife during a moderate event. The arc was visible to the eye, while the pillars were much clearer on camera. Sightings were reported as far south as Northumberland, the Pennines and north Wales at around this time.

TERMINOLOGY IN AURORA PREDICTIONS

As indicated in the box below, many alerting services are available to help with seeing the Northern Lights so it is useful to have a basic knowledge of their terminology. However, rest assured that you don't need to understand the detail. For a quick summary jump to 'Putting it all together' on pages 69–70.

One to four days ahead

For non-specialists, the first hints that a strong aurora may occur usually come from space weather prediction services. The term 'space weather' was first coined in the 1950s to describe variations in the solar wind, magnetic fields and radiation, and these services now operate in several countries to anticipate the potential for disruption to satellite, power and communication systems.

The predictions are usually based on observations of visible light and other electromagnetic activity on the sun, such as from the NASA/ESA Solar

ALERTING SERVICES AND FORUMS

Several smartphone and desktop apps are now available to help with spotting the Northern Lights; find them by searching online using terms like 'aurora alert' or 'aurora forecast'.

Their main purpose is usually to collect information from a wide range of ground-based and satellite observations and present it in a user-friendly way. Some include predictions based on the developer's own research. As always, it is worth doing some research first before deciding which app best meets your needs and budget, including whether they are specifically tailored to the British Isles. Also consider using the Met Office's Space Weather specialist forecasts and NOAA's Space Weather Enthusiast's Dashboard.

More generally, social media enables you to discuss sightings with fellow enthusiasts as an event develops, and this is one area where it excels. In the UK, popular groups include Aurora UK, Aurora Hunters UK, Aurora Watch UK, Cumbria Aurora and Glendale Skye Auroras. The tone is generally friendly and supportive, with people often happy to share their sightings and experience. Some aurora watchers join more than one group to get a range of tips on aurora hunting.

and Heliospheric Observatory (SOHO) satellite. Remarkably, due to the great distance of the sun from the Earth, it takes about eight minutes for radiation to be detected despite travelling at the speed of light.

Events that can often be seen include Coronal Mass Ejections (CMEs), solar flares and coronal holes. CMEs heading directly for the Earth are sometimes called 'halo' or 'full halo' events, based on how they appear on imaging sensors, although a glancing blow can also cause aurora. Sunspot activity can also be observed, and even predicted days ahead due to the rotation of the sun. These various observations are then used as inputs to sophisticated magnetohydrodynamic computer models. These cover an area known as the heliosphere, which extends way beyond the Earth and marks the extent of the sun's influence.

The first space weather prediction service was that of NOAA's Space Weather Prediction Center (SWPC). This is one of three space weather operations centres worldwide, the others being those of the US Air Force and the UK's Met Office. NOAA's 'Space Weather Enthusiasts Dashboard' is widely used by aurora enthusiasts. It includes a forecaster's written description of the potential for geomagnetic storms and a range of graphical and map-based outputs. Visualisations from a model called WSA-Enlil even include the predicted shapes and path of CMEs as they travel through the solar system, in addition to the path of the solar wind. The experimental 'Aurora Dashboard' on the same site provides a convenient, simpler summary of key information.

Predictions for the so-called planetary K index (Kp) are also useful and are given for the next two to three days. These give an indication of the strength of the expected magnetic field disturbance at the Earth's surface. As a side benefit, they provide an indication of the latitudes at which an aurora might be sighted; for example, values of 4–5 or more are often said to show potential for the northern British Isles. However, this is only a rough guide and those capricious lights often buck the trend. The Met Office's Space Weather specialist forecasts include predicted Kp outputs too.

About an hour to go

For non-specialists, the first confirmation of the accuracy of predictions is usually from two of the satellites that NOAA uses to study and monitor the space environment. These are the Advanced Composition Explorer (ACE) and its successor, the Deep Space Climate Observatory (DSCOVR). Both orbit the sun at the same rate as the Earth because they are placed near a point in space where the gravitational pulls of the sun and the Earth are roughly equal. This is known as Lagrange Point L1 and is just under a million miles from the Earth. ACE was launched in 1997 and now acts as a backup to DSCOVR, which began operation in 2015. The SOHO satellite is nearby. Some of these outputs appear on the SWPC dashboard or under the heading 'Real Time Solar Wind', reached via the main website.

During a strong display of the Northern Lights, solar wind speeds can reach several million miles per hour and CMEs sometimes travel at these speeds too. This can mean that an incoming event may only be detected an hour or less before it begins, which is why aurora watchers need to be ready to head out at short notice. However, it can take time for a display to build so, if conditions look particularly promising, some enthusiasts will take a chance and head out earlier based on space weather forecasts.

For the keen aurora watcher, useful parameters to monitor include the speed and density of the solar wind and the total strength of the interplanetary magnetic field (Bt) and its north–south component (Bz). High speeds and strengths imply more energy and high densities more particles. In particular, Bz is widely mentioned in alerting applications and on forums, and you will occasionally see the comment that it has 'flipped' or 'gone south'. This means that it is acting in opposition to the Earth's magnetic field at the geomagnetic north pole, making conditions promising for a good auroral display. The unit used for magnetic field strength is the nanoTesla (nT).

It's happening now

Once a storm arrives it is first detected by geostationary satellites, whose orbit at about 35,700km (22,300 miles) above the Earth makes them appear to hang stationary in space. The SWPC dashboard again helps by showing current outputs from NOAA GOES satellites and 'Probability of Aurora' forecasts for the next 30–40 minutes.

These forecasts are based on a computer model called the OVATION Aurora Model and show the probability that an aurora will be overhead on a scale of 0 to >4. The outputs are presented as an animation that includes the past 24 hours and are colour-coded, with red highlighting the most likely areas to be affected. For an aurora enthusiast it is particularly promising if an orange or red shaded area is heading your way. In practice, though, the lights are often still visible when viewed at an angle from the British Isles.

Ground-based magnetometers provide another useful source of information. These are typically operated by universities and national geophysical centres, and measure the magnetic field at the Earth's surface. So-called 'stack plots' from different latitudes are particularly useful to assess the progression of disturbances south. In the UK, the British Geological Survey and Lancaster University both publish outputs to their websites, while in Norway the Tromsø Geophysical Observatory helpfully brings together observations from several countries in and around the Arctic Circle.

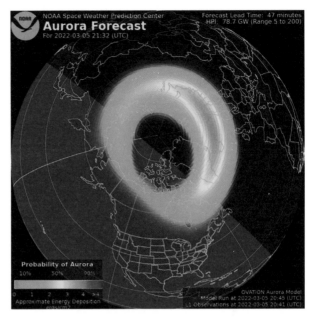

RIGHT An example of the output from NOAA's OVATION model for the northern hemisphere; although the green-coloured area only grazes northern Scotland good displays were seen in northern England and Scotland at about this time. © NOAA

Experts look at current and recent trends to build up a picture of what might happen next, and some organisations publish initial estimates for the observed planetary K index based on a weighted average of instruments around the world. As part of these calculations, the values from each instrument are scaled first to account for local variations in the strength of the Earth's magnetic field. However, in contrast to the predicted values mentioned earlier, these are less useful as by definition Kp is calculated as an average value for the past three hours. This can mean that the instantaneous peak has passed long before a high value is reported.

For scientific research, definitive values are published some time later by the German Research Centre for Geosciences (GFZ) in Potsdam, based on the outputs from 13 geomagnetic observatories around the world. These supersede the initial estimates made as an event is developing.

Putting it all together

Given all this information, you may be wondering how to use it. As with any such endeavour, it takes some experimentation, but a typical approach might be to keep an eye on alerting services and the NOAA SWPC and/or Met Office forecasts, maybe by checking them once a day. Watch weather forecasts, too, for the day or days in question.

Then, as the time approaches, if skies are likely to be clear and the moon not too bright, start checking your favourite alerting service(s) in more detail for current predictions, ready for a rapid departure if things suddenly improve. However, be aware that things can change quickly due to variations in the speed, density and magnetic field of the solar wind and CMEs.

As an event occurs, social media becomes particularly useful as you hear reports of sightings from other places around the British Isles. In particular, reports from areas further south are encouraging, even if you can't yet see any sign of the lights. And if you'd like to see for yourself how things are progressing, try the fabulous webcam images from the aurora camera at Eshaness Lighthouse in the Shetland Islands.

NOCTILUCENT CLOUDS

As summer approaches, another spectacle brightens the night skies, that of noctilucent clouds. These are high-altitude clouds that reflect the light of the sun after it has set at ground level but is still reaching higher altitudes. Typically, they appear as wispy, billowing streaks, mainly in silver or electric blue but sometimes with yellow and orange hues. Some displays have beautiful cross-hatch and waffle-like patterns.

BELOW The Northern Lights at about 4am near Loch Leven in Scotland, showing a green glow visible to the naked eye, with red and pink pillars rising above, visible on camera. Social media reports at around that time included sightings from Morecambe, Loch Lomond, Shetland and Skye. The bright lights on the horizon are from the city of Perth, about 32km (20 miles) to the north.

ABOVE Noctilucent clouds glowing above yacht masts after midnight in early June at a harbour in southeast Scotland.

The clouds are formed from ice crystals and occur at a height of about 80km (50 miles) in a layer of the atmosphere known as the mesosphere. They are therefore also called polar mesospheric clouds or night-shining clouds, when translated from the Latin. Like most clouds, they require dust or nuclei to form and at these great heights theories for their sources include volcanic dust, meteor trails, space dust and atmospheric pollution. Since they were first recorded scientifically in the 19th century, observations seem to have become more frequent, leading some scientists to speculate that this is linked to climate change.

The prime viewing time is around the summer equinox when the sun dips the least below the horizon. In the British Isles, they are most likely to be seen between late May and the end of July. Normally the best chance of a sighting is to look towards the north on a clear night, starting shortly before midnight. For specialists, clues to the formation of noctilucent clouds include high altitude (mesospheric) radar reflections recorded by ground- and satellite-based instruments and sightings by observers and webcams in countries to the east where night is further advanced, such as in Germany and the Netherlands. Sometimes noctilucent clouds are mentioned by aurora groups and alerting systems are starting to appear in smartphone apps, so watch out for when these become widely available.

Locations known for spectacular weather events

Gliding centres

Cairngorms National Park

Aboyne

Loch Lomond & the Trossachs National Park

Portmoak

Northumberland National Park

Cross Fell

North York Moors National Park

Lake District National Park

Yorkshire Dales National Park

Peak District National Park

Lleweni Parc

Snowdonia National Park

Bannau Brycheiniog National Park

Exmoor National Park

South Downs National Park

Dartmoor National Park

WEATHER

CHAPTER 4

HIDDEN CURRENTS

*See hawks climb in rising air and marvel at the
power of a thunderstorm. Spot mountain peaks floating
above a sea of cloud and valleys full of morning mist.*

Highlights

◆
**Wonder at the
massive forces in a
thunderstorm**

◆
**See mountain
peaks rise from a
sea of cloud**

◆
**Watch tendrils
of mist flow along a
mountain valley**

What you might see

As the sun rises the land warms, generating powerful currents of rising air invisible to the eye. However, clouds often give a clue to their presence, forming beautiful shifting shapes in the sky. The most dramatic occur during thunderstorms, with the cloud seeming to boil as it rises. Air is sometimes drawn in from miles around, with lightning adding to the display.

During times of high pressure, cloud is sometimes trapped beneath a warmer layer, giving rise to a white sea topped by blue sky. This is particularly spectacular to see from a mountain top if hills or peaks rise above.

As winter approaches, mist can add an air of mystery and beauty to even the most ordinary of scenes.

Level of difficulty ★★★

LOCATION widespread, although depends on the type of phenomenon
FREQUENCY ranges from seasonally to only every few years
PREDICTABILITY difficult to predict, although weather forecasts help
SAFETY normal outdoor risks, but particular care required in thunderstorms

Level ★★ for thunderstorms, Level ★★★ for picturesque mist,
Level ★★★★★ for inversions

OPPOSITE A rain cloud passing in front of Arthur's Seat in Edinburgh, with towering cumulus clouds behind.

PREVIOUS PAGES Low level mist in the Langdale Valley in the Lake District.

THUNDERY SHOWERS

One of the pleasures of a hot summer day is to lie back and watch the clouds as they drift across the sky. Some of the most familiar are the puffy white fair-weather clouds known as cumulus. These form on top of invisible rising currents called thermals, which can be imagined as huge bubbles of air released from areas warmed by the sun, such as bare fields and tarmac. Sometimes they organise into long parallel lines marching across the sky, separated by descending air. Glider pilots and soaring birds can ride the resulting cloud streets for miles.

On some days these innocuous looking clouds grow darker, forming giant swirling masses with a characteristic cauliflower shape to the top. These can rise to great heights, sometimes with long trailing anvils of cloud spreading across the sky. With their dark foreboding bases, these cumulonimbus clouds are a truly impressive sight.

When lightning occurs, thunder usually follows soon after, another sign of a thunderstorm nearby. Meteorologists estimate that at any one time more than 1,000 thunderstorms are occurring around the world, with more than a billion lightning strikes a year. The most intense are called supercells and

BELOW An active mass of cloud in a developing cumulonimbus cloud in northwest England.

OPPOSITE A circling buzzard in Pembrokeshire. Some birds of prey are masters at finding thermal lift and their circling and climbing is a good clue to its presence.

have a deep, rising rotating core. These are common in the interior plains of the USA and sometimes spawn tornadoes, particularly in Tornado Alley, which stretches roughly northward from Texas to South Dakota. This area is a magnet for storm chasers and featured in the 1996 blockbuster movie *Twister*. Although rare, supercells occasionally occur in the UK when the air is unusually unstable.

Thunderstorms last an hour or so in the UK but can rumble on longer if they spawn new storm cells. These massive structures can exceed 16km (10 miles) across at the base and rise 30,000ft or more into the sky. They often occur as the weather 'breaks down' after a spell of unusually warm weather.

Severe Weather Warnings issued by the Met Office provide one of the best indications that they may occur in the next few hours. Warnings are colour-coded yellow, amber or red in increasing order of severity, as in the following example from the Met Office on 5 June 2022:

> *A yellow National Severe Weather Warning for thunderstorms covering the southern half of Wales, the southern Midlands and parts of southwest England is valid from 1pm until late this evening with some travel disruption and localised flooding possible.*

Warnings are initially fairly general in terms of location and timing, but more information becomes available nearer the time. Some sensible advice is to only venture outside if strictly necessary and to keep away from hilltops, open spaces and masts. Hail is another potential hazard, with the largest recorded hailstone in the UK more than 50mm (2in) across, capable of damaging car windscreens and house windows. Nearer the time, television and online video forecasts become increasingly useful as they include the expert opinion of the forecaster. Map-based online forecasts are also useful, such as the rainfall layer in the Met Office's UK Weather Map, which gives a pictorial representation of where rain is expected.

Thunder provides another major clue, of course, as it is typically only heard when a storm is within about 15–20km (10–12 miles) of your location. If you spot lightning, start counting in seconds because you can estimate a storm's distance in miles by dividing the time delay to thunder by five. For example, if the time between lightning and thunder is 11 seconds, the storm is just over two miles away.

Why do thunderstorms occur?

When it is hot outside, hill and mountain tops often provide a welcome retreat from the heat. This is because air temperature normally decreases with height. The rate of decrease is called the lapse rate and in the UK is typically in the range 5–10°C per thousand metres, or about 1.5–3°C per thousand feet.

Thermals tend to rise more quickly when the lapse rate is high, a sign that the air is unstable. However, rising air expands due to the decrease in air pressure, causing it to cool and water vapour to eventually condense, forming masses of tiny water droplets that become cloud. These drops are normally smaller than the thickness of a human hair and form around even smaller nuclei, such as particles of dust, salt from sea spray, or smoke and ash from fires.

Due to this temperature dependence, cumulus clouds often tend to rise upwards from a similar altitude, known as the cloud base. This is typically around 2,000–3,000ft on a summer's day in the UK, although may reach 5,000ft or more on a hot summer's afternoon.

Condensation also releases energy, so in the right conditions a cloud will continue to grow, as long as there is a ready supply of moisture from below. Sometimes this leads to towering cumulus clouds, rising high in the sky. These often appear brilliant white when in sunshine and can be fascinating to watch as they boil and grow, particularly when viewed with binoculars. In the tropics, some clouds reach heights of 15,000m (50,000ft) or more, higher than most jet airliners fly, and heights greater than 9,000m (30,000ft) are possible in the UK. Night flights in the tropics can be particularly spectacular as the pilot flies a slalom course to avoid vast towers of cloud, lit up inside like Chinese lanterns.

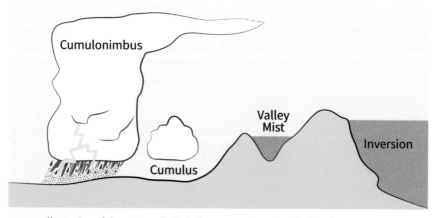

ABOVE Illustration of the meteorological phenomena described in this chapter.

HOW MUCH DOES A CLOUD WEIGH?

Have you ever wondered how much a cloud weighs? This depends on its type and size, of course, but the Met Office provides the following answer in the book *Very British Weather: over 365 Hidden Wonders from the World's Greatest Forecasters*:

While there are many factors that will determine the exact amount of moisture a cloud can hold – including temperature, altitude and pressure – we can work with an estimate of about 0.5 grams of water per cubic metre for the average cumulus cloud. This means an average-sized cumulus cloud would weigh about 400,000 kilograms, roughly the same as an Airbus A380.

Lightning occurs due to collisions between rising ice particles and larger falling particles, such as hail. Electrons ripped off the smaller particles are carried down into the lowermost parts of the cloud, which becomes increasingly negatively charged. This in turn repels electrons from the ground immediately below, making the ground positively charged, along with the top of the cloud.

As charge continues to build, this sets the scene for one of the most spectacular types of lightning: cloud-to-ground lightning. This occurs when a narrow channel of ionised gas or plasma opens up briefly between cloud and ground, often to a mast, mountain top or other prominent feature. The lightning we see consists of pulses or strokes of electrical discharge heading skyward in the opposite direction, moving so fast that the eye cannot make out each of the individual strokes. Other types of lightning include cloud lightning, sheet lightning and the very rare ball lightning.

Thunder results from the shockwaves caused by the sudden expansion of air due to the heat generated by lightning. Typically this is heard as a rumbling noise when a storm is in the distance and a loud crack if it is close by. In some storms, extraordinary looking mammatus or mamma clouds form beneath the anvil, as cool air drops down through warmer rising air. Their name was inspired by their globular shape, and is derived from the Latin word for udders. Tubular and pouch shapes also occur. These are sometimes seen in the UK, for example during Storm Dudley in 2022 when awestruck weather enthusiasts in Scotland shared images of mammatus on social media.

WEATHER WATCHING TIPS

Perhaps more than any topic in this book, weather watching is as much about having the right approach as knowing when and where to go, over time becoming more in tune with the weather and the viewing opportunities that arise.

In a fascinating presentation on weather photography for the Royal Meteorological Society, meteorologist Matt Clark gave the following great tip:

> *These kinds of features range from relatively common to extremely rare so you never quite know what you're going to see. I think these things demonstrate in particular why it's really worth having your camera with you all the time because you just don't know when you're going to see them and it's often opportunistic; you just have to take them wherever you are. So you'll see with some of these photos that they're not beautifully sort of posed with really nice backgrounds, it's just a case of getting the phenomenon when it occurs.*

Matt is a Met Office researcher and was Photo Editor for *Weather Magazine* for five years. Here he was talking about spotting rainbows and other optical phenomena, but this approach could apply to many other types of weather too.

One step towards success can be to make slight modifications to your daily schedule. For example, if conditions look promising, try leaving early for work to pass a local viewpoint, or take an evening walk or cycle ride rather than staying in. Similarly, while on holiday an early start or a slight change to plans may yield dividends, particularly if out hill or coastal walking.

Another tip is to get into the habit of checking the weather forecast every day to see if anything interesting might occur. Forecasters may drop useful clues, such as 'cloud will bubble up during the day' or 'following a misty start, skies are expected to clear by mid-morning'. Longer-range forecasts help too, including the 3–5-day forecasts from the Met Office, the 'Weather for the week ahead' from the BBC, and those from the Mountain Weather Information Service (MWIS).

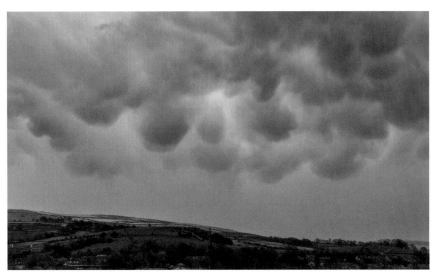

ABOVE Extreme weather with cumulonimbus and mammatus clouds above the northern town of New Mills in Derbyshire. © Getty/John Finney Photography

CLOUD RECOGNITION

When out watching clouds, it helps to have a basic understanding of the terms used by forecasters. These are usually as defined in the World Meteorological Organization's International Cloud Atlas and consist of general names (or genera) and species. Additional terms are sometimes added to note the variety of a cloud and any supplementary features.

General names include cumulus, cirrus and the rather less interesting stratus, which typically form layers across the sky. There are ten genera in total, grouped according to whether they are normally found at Low, Middle or High altitudes.

Taking cumulus clouds as an example, an actively growing cloud taller than it is wide would be called *Cumulus congestus*. The variety *radiatus* would be added if it is forming cloud streets (*Cumulus radiatus*). If it continues growing it would eventually be redefined as a cumulonimbus cloud, of which the most common type is *Cumulonimbus capillatus*. The supplementary feature *mamma* would be added if mammatus clouds form and *incus* if it has an anvil. Thus, a *Cumulonimbus capillatus incus mamma* cloud would have both anvil and mamma features.

These various names are derived from Latin: for example, loosely translated, cirrus means curl or tuft, cumulus means heap or pile, and nimbus means rain-bearing. Colloquial names include mares' tails for cirrus and fair-weather clouds for cumulus. More generally, since cumulus clouds are caused by rising warm air, they are classed as a type of convective cloud, whereas those caused by the flow of air past hills and mountains are known as orographic clouds, as described in the next chapter.

The World Meteorological Organization website gives a handy interactive guide to the Atlas. Other good places to learn more about clouds include the websites of the Met Office, Royal Meteorological Society and the Mountain Weather Information Service, and the Further reading section of this book. The Royal Meteorological Society and the Tornado and Storm Research Organisation (TORRO) both welcome keen enthusiasts as does the Cloud Appreciation Society, which has members from more than 100 countries interested in the scientific and artistic aspects of clouds.

BELOW Three main types of cloud are visible in this coastal view, which from top to bottom are of the genera cirrus, stratus and cumulus. Cirrus clouds are formed from ice crystals and can be a sign of an approaching warm front, sometimes with hook shapes followed by lines stretched out along the direction of the wind. As the front approaches, they are often followed by ever-lowering layers of cloud and heavy rain.

ABOVE An inversion in the Scottish Highlands.

INVERSIONS, FOG AND MIST

Inversions

Following periods of rain and wind, a brief lull is often a pleasure, especially when winds become calm and skies clear. These periods are often associated with high pressure and sometimes last for days. Weather forecasters may refer to a dome of high pressure building over the UK or the whole of Europe. These conditions are ripe for one of the most beautiful and difficult-to-forecast signs of hidden currents. Called a temperature inversion, it appears as a sea of cloud, sometimes at heights of just a few hundred feet.

At ground level, conditions may be hazy and overcast, but in mountain areas the sense can be magical as other peaks poke out of the mist or fog like islands, floating above a sea of white. These effects are sometimes seen in lower lying country if you can get up to heights of a few hundred feet or more, such as on Dartmoor or in the Peak District. Airline passengers sometimes see inversions too, as the aircraft pops up out of the murk into blue skies.

Inversions normally occur when air descends, warming as it goes, forming a thin layer of more stable air above the colder layer near the ground. This can trap a layer of cloud and mist below, and sometimes air pollution too, giving the air a brownish tinge.

A VIEW FROM ON HIGH

Since becoming popular in the 1980s, paragliding has come a long way, with pilots achieving great distances powered only by rising currents of air. Using only a wing that can be carried on your back, it is perhaps the most accessible form of aviation. The website of the British Hang Gliding and Paragliding Association (BHPA) expresses this well:

Imagine parking your car at a beautiful upland vantage point on a sparkling spring day. You open the boot and don flying suit and boots, then lift out your incredibly light flying machine in its carrying rucksack and trek off a few yards to where your friends are preparing to fly. After a few minutes spent inspecting your equipment you put on your helmet and harness, look around, allow the wind to raise the canopy of your glider and launch off into space. This is paragliding…

Many paraglider pilots strive to perfect their skills in cross-country flying. A summer sky filled with fluffy cumulus clouds provides abundant – but invisible – lifting currents which pilots use to gain altitude. Setting off on such a day, either towards a pre-selected goal or just drifting where the wind will take you, is one of the most breathtaking experiences available today. Most pilots will talk of the sense of privilege they feel when drifting from cloud to cloud, in almost total silence, watching the landscape unfold beneath them as they navigate across the sky.

Training is essential and it normally takes several flying days or more to achieve the basic qualification, beyond which, there is still much to learn. When flying cross country, the ability to read the sky is crucial; pilots must constantly try to spot the best clouds within flying distance and other clues to rising air, such as circling birds of prey. On reaching cloud base, once the lift decreases it's time to fly as fast as possible to the next source, by attempting to visualise where the next thermal is likely to be. On finding lift, it's then time to slow down and start circling again to find the strongest core. Cloud streets make life easier by offering a line of clouds to follow, provided, of course, that they are heading in the right direction.

In the UK, hike and fly events are becoming increasingly popular, with pilots achieving huge distances in mountain areas, such as the Lake District, Wales and Scotland. More generally, the current UK record for straight-line distance flight is more than 300km (186 miles).

LEFT One of the joys of paragliding: climbing in a thermal on a cross-country flight on a beautiful summer day, all the while scanning the sky ahead for the next source of lift. © Fly with Greg; Greg Hamerton

Inversions are typically associated with slow moving or stationary areas of high pressure, with a steady supply of moist air, such as from the sea, and light winds, with no storms or weather fronts to affect the cloud. However, the inversion height is difficult to predict so, even if conditions are promising, hill tops may still be covered, which has spoiled many a hillwalker's view. You are most likely to see an inversion in autumn or winter as water vapour is more likely to condense in the cooler air, but they occur in spring and summer too.

Fog and mist

Less dramatic perhaps, but still beautiful at times, fog and mist can form wonderful patterns, wreathing buildings, trees and hills in an otherworldly charm. Perhaps the best-known type is radiation fog, which typically forms on clear nights as the ground cools due to infrared radiation causing air near the surface to cool too, sometimes enough for mist to form. A light breeze helps to mix up the air, allowing the layer to grow, provided that the motion is not strong enough to cause it to dissipate. The mist normally burns off in the morning sun, although it can linger all day. Radiation fog is best seen in autumn and winter around lakes, canals, rivers and reservoirs, where there is a ready supply of moist air.

In the mountains, valley fog sometimes arises at night for similar reasons as cooler mountain air flows downhill to be trapped by the surrounding hills and ridges. This density-driven flow is known as a katabatic wind. For both types, an early morning walk can pay dividends, along with getting to know the best places to visit in your local area.

The words mist and fog are often used interchangeably, but meteorologists use visibility criteria to define the difference. In aviation, the boundary is at a visibility of 1km, whereas a slightly looser definition is used in public weather forecasts, with fog typically being declared when visibility is less than about 100–200m.

In addition to radiation and valley fog, other types include upslope fog, which occurs on hill and mountain slopes, and advection fog, which occurs when warm, moist air crosses a cooler surface, such as a lake or the sea. One type of advection fog even has its own local name and is described in the chapter on named winds and weather on page 113. More unusually, evaporation fog can occur with lake and river surfaces seeming to boil in weak sunlight as cooler air passes over above. Also called steam fog, this is most likely in high latitude regions.

BELOW Early morning fog at Grasmere in the Lake District; the tendril of mist to the right of the image was slowly flowing up the side valley.

CHAPTER 5

MOUNTAIN CLOUDS

*See mysterious lens shaped clouds in the mountains,
sometimes resembling flying saucers. Try to spot a peak with
a cap of cloud or trailing a banner behind.*

Highlights

◆
View lens-shaped
clouds marching off
into the distance

◆
Spot strange UFO-
shaped clouds glowing
in the evening sun

◆
Try to spot a
smoking mountain or
a mountain capped
by cloud

What you might see

When strong winds blow, the air twists and turns around any hills and
mountains in its path. When conditions are right, truly spectacular cloud
formations can occur, such as lens-shaped clouds that march off downwind

WEATHER

and are known as lenticular clouds. Cap clouds sometimes form too, seeming to cling to a ridge or mountain top, along with banner clouds, which trail downwind like an unfurled flag.

Some are downright strange, most notably when lenticular clouds pile one on top of another, forming huge ephemeral shapes that are sometimes mistaken for flying saucers.

———————————————— Level of difficulty ★★★★ ————————————————

LOCATION primarily in mountain areas, but sometimes near lower hills
FREQUENCY typically several times a year at suitable locations
PREDICTABILITY difficult to predict; specialised weather forecasts help
SAFETY normal outdoor risks, with particular care required in strong winds

Level ★★★ for lenticular clouds, Level ★★★★ for a pile d'assiettes, Level ★★★★★ for cap and banner clouds

ABOVE A mysterious 'spaceship' shaped cloud arrives over Morecambe Bay.

MOUNTAIN WEATHER

In mountain areas the weather can be a source of joy, with magnificent cloudscapes and ever-changing light. In poor conditions, though, everything seems more extreme, with buffeting winds and limited visibility. Pilots keep a respectful distance and most keen hillwalkers will have experienced winds that could knock them off their feet.

These conditions occur because as the wind flows over a mountain range it either has to find its way through valleys or rise over the top. As it twists and turns, this sometimes gives rise to the unusual cloudscapes described in this chapter. Examples include lenticular clouds that form in waves triggered as air is forced upwards over a mountain range, and cap clouds that cling to its peaks. Dramatic banner clouds sometimes form too, trailing like an unfurled flag or banner downwind of a peak. These various phenomena differ from the more familiar cumulus clouds that form in calmer conditions, and the beautiful mists and cloudscapes of valley fog and inversions, described in the chapter on Hidden Currents.

LENTICULAR CLOUDS

Lenticular clouds typically occur on the lee (downwind) side of a mountain range, and are often elongated and smooth-edged, resembling a camera lens,

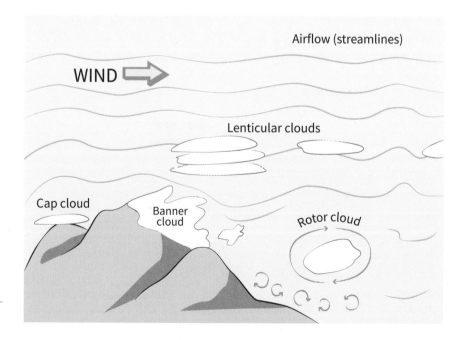

lentil or almond. They often persist for many miles, with each cloud roughly parallel to the range with gaps of clear air in between. Satellite images have shown that they sometimes extend over huge distances, including from Ireland to the North Sea or from Scotland to northern England.

These clouds are caused by atmospheric gravity waves, triggered when the wind crosses a hill or mountain range, which are often called mountain or lee waves. One way to visualise them is to think of the waves that form behind a rock just below a river surface in a fast-moving stream. Here an initial wave on the surface is followed by a train of smaller waves heading downstream. The 'whelps' that follow a tidal bore have some similarities, as shown in the photograph on page 121.

The shape of a hill or mountain range also has an effect, as the air needs to be given enough of an upwards push, but not too much. The strongest waves therefore occur with moderate slopes in the windward direction since a sharp ridge gives too big a jolt and a long, smoothly sloping ridge not enough.

In contrast to most other types of cloud, lenticular clouds remain roughly stationary relative to the ground rather than being blown with the wind. However, if you look closely, they constantly reform on the upwind side as moisture condenses in the rising air, then dissipate on the downwind side through evaporation. This is perhaps easiest to see through binoculars and you can find some excellent time-lapse videos online. The most usual form

OPPOSITE Illustration of the formation of lenticular, cap, banner and rotor clouds.

ABOVE Tendrils of cloud near Ben Nevis in Scotland, the highest peak in the British Isles.

is called *Altocumulus lenticularis*, although *stratocumulus* and *cirrocumulus* versions also occur.

Occasionally lenticular clouds pile up on top of one another, so that viewed side-on they look like a single cloud with several sharp-edged layers. Meteorologists add the variety *duplicatus* when this occurs, but they are also known colloquially as a *pile d'assiettes* from the French for a pile or stack of plates. Some look like a cartoon version of a spaceship or flying saucer, particularly in the glow of the setting sun. This has led to quite a few reports of UFO sightings over the years, with Mount Rainier in the USA one famed location.

Lower down, strongly rotating areas of turbulent air may form, sometimes with wispy cloud giving its presence away. This is known as rotor and is given a wide berth by light aircraft due to the violent turbulence that can occur.

When do lenticular clouds form?

Lenticular clouds are most likely to occur in a well-developed mountain wave system, which typically forms when a strong wind meets a mountain range more or less head on. Chances improve if winds are stronger higher up, and a temperature inversion on or above mountain tops can help too.

In his classic book *Meteorology for Glider Pilots*, CE Wallington provides more technical detail, saying that:

> *Conditions favourable for lee waves with appreciable vertical currents comprise:*

ABOVE Lenticular clouds on a windy day near Ben Lawers at Loch Tay in Scotland.

BELOW Altocumulus lenticularis clouds over and immediately to the lee of the Yorkshire Pennines. The clouds formed in a stable west to southwesterly wind and persisted for several hours. Cloud base was about 17,000–18,000ft with tops of 20,000–25,000ft and the largest was about 20–30km (12–19 miles) east of the highest peaks. © Matthew Clark, 2011

1 A layer of low stability (high lapse rate) at low levels
2 A stable layer (e.g. isothermal layer or inversion) above the lower layer
3 An upper layer of low stability in the troposphere
4 A wind of about 15kts (30km/h) or more across a hill or mountain ridge...

An increase of wind speed with height without much change of wind direction adds to the likelihood of wave formation.

(The terms lapse rate and inversion are explained on pages 78 and 83 respectively.)

The size of a lenticular cloud depends on both wind speeds and stability, and under typical British conditions they can reach heights of 10,000–20,000ft or more.

Other types of atmospheric waves

While mountain waves are the best known, several other types occur in the atmosphere. However, they are usually caused by low level currents or sudden variations in wind speed, rather than uplift over a mountain range.

Roll clouds are one spectacular example. As their name suggests, they are long rolling clouds that line up at low level across the wind direction. They occur in stable air and are often associated with sea breeze fronts, which occur when rising air inland draws in air from the sea. Worldwide they are rare, but due to unique local conditions happen several times a year near the Gulf of Carpentaria in Australia. Here they are called Morning Glories and are a popular soaring challenge for glider pilots. Sequences of clouds several hundred miles long have been observed.

On a much smaller scale, Kelvin Helmholtz waves are named after two eminent 19th-century physicists. They are a type of billow cloud and occur when a faster moving air mass passes over a slower layer of air. From the side their appearance is similar to the classic shape of a breaking wave in the sea, each rising to a crest before spilling over into the air below. Occasionally seen in the UK, they are typically only a few hundred feet high and last at best a few minutes.

Mackerel skies are much more common and consist of altocumulus or cirrocumulus cloud broken up by high altitude atmospheric waves. With a billowing, rippling appearance, in gentle evening sunlight they can take on a beautiful red glow. At even higher altitudes, rare nacreous clouds sometimes form in the stratosphere in polar regions. Also known as 'mother-of-pearl'

OPPOSITE A glider approaching to land at the Scottish Gliding Centre airfield at Portmoak on a great day for wave flying.

RIDING THE MOUNTAIN WAVES

While many pilots give mountains a wide berth in strong winds, some glider pilots have become experts at riding mountain waves. Potential hazards include extreme cold, massive downdrafts and the cloud closing in below. It is an extreme but beautiful form of flying that requires great skill to accomplish.

Huge height gains are possible and the world record stands at about 76,000ft roughly twice the cruising altitude of a jet airliner. This was achieved by Jim Payne and Tim Gardner in the Andes in 2018, in the experimental sailplane *Perlan 2*. To achieve this great height, they took advantage of a rare form of lift called stratospheric wave, which only occurs in subpolar regions a few times a year. The Perlan project hopes to eventually get a glider to a height of 90,000ft.

In the UK, heights of more than 30,000ft have been achieved and glider pilots regularly fly distances of more than 500km (311 miles) using mountain waves, averaging speeds of 160km/h (100mph) or more. Start points for record flights have included Portmoak, Aboyne and Lleweni Parc airfields, homes of the Scottish Gliding Centre, the Deeside Gliding Club and Denbigh Gliding.

One such expert is Sant Cervantes, who flies from Portmoak and holds five gliding records. Following a 1,000km (621-mile) flight, he gave the

following insights to the BBC in an article titled 'The glider pilots surfing the skies over Scotland':

Your glider is an extension of your personality... What you've got out there is an ocean of air and each day is different. It's a voyage of discovery – of the sky and yourself... If you're competent then you get in the zone like an athlete. You've got the conditions, you've got the glider and you've got yourself. When you get it right you feel like you're in harmony with the environment. You're on a knife edge and you just shoot along. It's fantastic.

In an article for *Sailplane & Gliding* magazine he added:

The forces in play are immense and the wave clouds have a stunning beauty and grace. In your glider you are but a speck in this infinite expanse.

To predict when conditions are right, pilots use both observations and forecasts to assess likely wind speeds, cloud cover and atmospheric stability. Sources of information include synoptic charts, satellite imagery and complex charts used to assess atmospheric conditions, known as tephigrams. Many also use a fabulous tool called Regional Atmospheric Soaring Prediction (RASP) which presents atmospheric model outputs using informative maps and graphs. For mountain wave predictions, the vertical velocity outputs for pressure levels of 850mb and 700mb are particularly useful, corresponding to heights of roughly 5,000ft and 10,000ft. The RASP approach was initially developed by meteorologist and gliding enthusiast Dr John (Jack) Glendening in the USA.

Mountain waves can form on surprisingly low hills, and even tops a few hundred feet high may be sufficient. To maximise the potential for long flights, gliding sites are often located in areas where waves occur, giving pilots an alternative to the other main ways of staying aloft, namely thermals and slope or ridge lift. With advance notice, most gliding clubs offer trial flights for visitors. In hilly areas you might be lucky and see lenticular clouds, or even get the chance to fly in mountain waves. See the British Gliding Association website for more details.

OPPOSITE A glider rides a mountain wave at an altitude of about 5,000ft during a flying lesson at the Scottish Gliding Centre at Portmoak. © NOAA

ABOVE Morning Glory cloud formation between Burketown and Normanton, Australia. © Wikimedia/Mick Petroff

BELOW Table Mountain with 'tablecloth', and 12 Apostles viewed from Lion's Head, Cape Town, South Africa. © Getty/Education Images/Universal Images Group

clouds or polar stratospheric clouds, due to their great height they remain briefly lit by the sun after dark, again with spectacular colours. Most common in winter, they are often linked to atmospheric gravity waves.

Others occur on a larger scale and are important to understand when developing weather forecasting and climate prediction models. Rossby waves are one example and arise from the influence of the rotation of the Earth on the atmosphere. Found at high altitudes at mid to high latitudes, they meander around the planet, influencing both the jet stream and storm paths, such as those which cross the Atlantic to our shores. Due to their grand scale, they are often called planetary waves.

Satellite observations are increasingly revealing wave activity perhaps only suspected in the past. Examples include cloud wakes streaming out downwind of island peaks, like the wake behind a boat, sometimes with rolling circular lines of vortices similar to those that stream out behind the tip of an aircraft wing.

MOUNTAIN CAP AND BANNER CLOUDS

When strong winds cross a peak, the uplift can cause cloud to form locally, capping the peak in cloud. Known as cap clouds, like lenticular clouds, these have smooth edges and constantly reform as moisture condenses on the upwind side and evaporates on the downwind side. They are sometimes of

ABOVE The Matterhorn with banner clouds framed by flowers at Riffelsee.
© Getty/Thomas Janisch

the type *Altocumulus lenticularis* and are sometimes called Foehn or Föhn walls when they lie along a ridge. They can be beautiful to look at from afar, but rob the hill walker of a view when approaching the summit. Various factors affect their size and formation, including the pooling of cooler air on the windward side, forcing warmer air to pass above it. They are often associated with lenticular clouds, but these do not have to occur for a cap cloud to appear.

One of the most famous is the 'tablecloth' cloud that forms over Table Mountain in South Africa. Cap clouds also occur in the UK, for example in the Cairngorms in Scotland, but much less frequently. The most famous British example is the Helm Cloud, which is described on page 105.

Sometimes the wind is so strong that a swirling mass of air forms behind the peak. This is rotor, which is highly dangerous to light aircraft. Due to a combination of low pressure and updrafts, some of the cloud that forms swirls back towards the peak, rotating in its wake.

In the right conditions, a rare type of cloud forms called banner cloud. This can look like an unfurled flag streaming out behind the mountain, with more ragged edges than a cap cloud due to the eddying nature of the flow. Sometimes a peak looks as if it is on fire and the term 'smoking mountain' is used, although this can also refer to a peak trailing a plume of driven snow in high winds.

The conditions for formation of banner clouds are not completely understood, but they are most likely to occur behind isolated peaks. Well-known examples include the Matterhorn, the Rock of Gibraltar and Mount Everest. Banner clouds occur occasionally in the Scottish Highlands downwind of isolated peaks and ridges.

On a much larger scale, the uplift of air over a mountain range can cause a rain shadow downwind if there is a prevailing wind. As it warms, the dry, descending air can lead to dramatic rises in air temperature at low level, and the resulting much drier areas sometimes extend for hundreds of miles, as seen in the prairies to the east of the Rocky Mountains. This effect is also common in the Alps, and occasionally occurs in the Scottish Highlands, causing drier and warmer weather to the east.

If you would like to try to spot cap and banner clouds, mountain weather forecasts give some clues. However, realistically they are most likely to be seen by chance by hillwalkers, skiers or climbers. For the armchair enthusiast, there are again some stunning time-lapse videos online of these amazing phenomena.

CHAPTER 6

NAMED WINDS AND WEATHER

See the mysterious clouds caused by Britain's only named wind, and feel its power on the valley floor. Learn how storms, and fog, can have names.

◆
Marvel at the
dramatic clouds
caused by Britain's
only named wind

◆
Watch out for the
next named storm

◆
Catch sea frets
and Haar rolling in
from the sea

What you might see

When an easterly wind blows over the North Pennines, a dramatic rolling cloud sometimes hovers above Cumbria's Eden Valley. This is due to Britain's

only named wind – the Helm – which can cause gusts at ground level strong enough to damage farm buildings. The Helm is one of a select band of named winds around the world that includes the Mistral of southern France, the Khamsin of North Africa and the Chinook of the USA.

Named storms can provide interesting viewing opportunities too, as can the sea fret and Haar fogs of northeast England and Scotland.

Level of difficulty	★★★★★

LOCATION the Helm only affects a specific area in Cumbria's Eden Valley
FREQUENCY typically a few times a year in the right conditions
PREDICTABILITY difficult to predict, although weather forecasts help
SAFETY normal outdoor risks, with particular care required in fog and strong winds

Level ★★★ for the Haar and sea frets, Level ★★★★★ for the Helm

BELOW The Helm Bar seen from near Hartside Pass in the North Pennines.

THE HELM

The open moorland of the North Pennines stretches north from the Yorkshire Dales to east of Carlisle. The highest point is Cross Fell (893m/2,930ft), whose rounded limestone mass is topped by an impressive cross-shaped shelter, built from stone typical of the drystone walls in this area. From the top there are expansive views west across the Eden Valley to the hills of the Lake District, whose tallest mountain, Scafell Pike, is only about 91m (300ft) feet higher. A short way southeast, Great Dun Fell (848m/2,782ft) is topped by the dome of a radar system that is visible for miles around.

The ridge remains above about 750m (2,500ft) for about 6km (4 miles), making it one of the longest and highest in England. To the west, it drops about 600m (2,000ft) into the Eden Valley. In a moderate westerly wind, glider pilots can spend hours soaring in the smooth lift this barrier generates.

However, when the wind blows from the east a most unusual phenomenon sometimes occurs in which air accelerates down to the valley floor. The Helm Wind, Britain's only named wind, can reach Force 9 (strong/severe gale force) near the top of the ridge and still be at Force 7–8 (gale force) lower down. This can damage farm buildings, crops and trees and – according to local folklore – even knock cows and sheep off their feet. In earlier times, horse-drawn carts would be blown over and haystacks tumble across fields.

ABOVE The distinctive radome on Great Dun Fell viewed from the Eden Valley. The radar equipment it protects helps air traffic controllers to monitor air traffic in the north of England and Scotland.

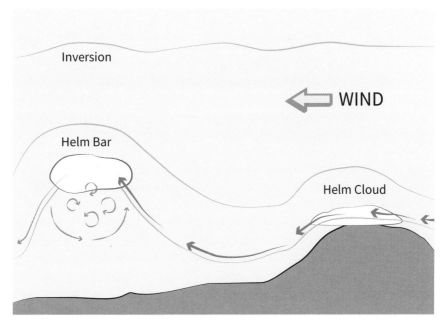

Inversion

WIND

Helm Bar

Helm Cloud

ABOVE Illustration of the conditions leading to formation of the Helm Cloud and the Helm Bar.

Sometimes the wind lasts for days and its noise has been compared to the rumble of distant thunder or the sea in a storm. The video for 'Helm Blues' by Cumbrian band Hereldeduke, which featured in an episode of the BBC series *Wild Weather*, gives you an idea of some of problems it causes!

A friendlier side sometimes emerges in the form of two spectacular clouds: the Helm Cloud and the Helm Bar. The Helm Cloud is a smooth-edged cloud that clings to the top of the ridge, and folklore suggests that its cap or helmet-like shape may have inspired the cloud's name. Less frequently, the Helm Bar forms three to four miles out in the Eden Valley. With its rolling cigar-like or cylindrical shape, this is a most unusual sight as it hovers above the ground, hardly moving with the wind. Sometimes it takes on an otherworldly appearance as its smooth white edges contrast with the blue of the skies around it. In the best conditions it is several miles long.

The Bar forms when the wind streaming down from the ridge shoots skyward again. This happens because a standing wave occurs – a distant relative of that formed when fast-flowing water falls from a tap on to the bottom of a sink. Meteorologically this is known as a rotor cloud, while the Helm Cloud is a type of cap cloud, as described on pages 99–100.

The Helm Bar forms as water vapour condenses in rising air downstream of the ridge. Typically, an area of blue sky separates it from the ridge where the air is descending, causing any cloud to evaporate. Once at ground level,

GORDON MANLEY AND THE TROUBLESOME WIND

Much of our scientific understanding of the Helm arises from research carried out in the 1930s by geographer Gordon Manley (1902–80) when he was working at Durham University. A keen hill walker, he made many trips across the Pennines in all weathers to collect meteorological data. This included changing mechanically driven chart recorders, as this was long before the days of digital data loggers.

The Royal Geographical Society, together with the Institute of British Geographers (IBG), has devised and created a fascinating trail telling the story of Gordon Manley. It is part of a fantastic project called Discovering Britain (www.discoveringbritain.org), which aims to bring geography alive for everyone by suggesting places to visit, trails and walks throughout the British Isles. This particular 10-mile (16km) round trip, known as 'Troublesome wind', starts from the village of Knock and goes as far as Great Dun Fell. The website shows the route and includes links to audio and written guides. These give many insights into the Helm, although the guide suggests that those planning to tackle the walk should be a more experienced walker and that 'The Helm Wind is both feared and celebrated by locals. If you think you can see this cloud forming now, it may be wise to descend!'

wind speeds reduce dramatically beneath the Bar and may even become calm. Lenticular clouds may form high above, as described on pages 90–94. Further west, the wind picks up speed to match that of the prevailing wind.

FINDING THE HELM

The weather in the North Pennines, as a high moorland region, varies from clear sunny days to violent storms with deep snow blanketing the hills. The Helm can occur at any time of year, but you are most likely to see it in spring and early summer, with autumn the next most frequent. In the right conditions it sometimes lasts for days.

On the valley floor, the villages most affected by the force of the wind lie in a narrow band near the foot of the ridge. Even in the strongest conditions, this is little more than a couple of miles wide, with its end points near the villages of Hilton and Renwick. However, the best places to really see the Helm clouds are to either side of its path, so it is worth exploring the roads nearby, such as near Culgaith and Temple Sowerby. Alternatively, for a

More generally, this is a great area to explore, which the website of the North Pennines AONB describes as 'a stunning landscape of open heather moors, dramatic dales, tumbling upland rivers, wonderful woods, close knit communities, glorious waterfalls, fantastic birds, colourful hay meadows, stone-built villages'. The Visit Eden website describes the many historic and scenic destinations in the Eden Valley to the west.

RIGHT The cover of *Troublesome wind: A self-guided walk in the North Pennines.* © Royal Geographical Society with IBG

DISCOVERING BRITAIN >

Royal Geographical Society
with IBG

Troublesome wind
A self guided walk in the North Pennines

Explore the spectacular scenery around Great Dun Fell
Discover why it experiences some of the most extreme weather in England
Hear some remarkable accounts of Britain's only named wind
Find out about one man's lifetime spent observing the weather

www.discoveringbritain.org
the stories of our landscapes
discovered through walks

higher view, Hartside Pass to the east reaches an elevation of 580m (1,904ft) if the pass is open and driving conditions allow.

The specialist mountain forecasts from the Met Office and the Mountain Weather Information Service sometimes give clues to the Helm's presence: for example, by mentioning gusty easterly winds on Cross Fell or powerful downslope gusts into the Eden Valley. A useful rule of thumb is to look for high pressure to the northeast combined with a steady east to north northeasterly (E to NNE) wind of at least 24–32km/h (15–20mph) to the east of the North Pennines. Ideally there should be a stable airflow capped by an inversion around 600-900m (2,000-3,000ft) above the ridge height.

If you would like to delve more into the meteorological aspects of the Helm, the RASP vertical velocity outputs mentioned on page 97 are useful, as are the wind speed and direction observations from the weather stations at Warcop and Great Dun Fell. Perhaps the definitive book on the topic is *The Anatomy of the Helm Wind* by David Uttley, which explores the social, cultural and historical aspects of the wind and gives a much more detailed meteorological explanation than is possible here.

NAMED STORMS

While we have been naming storms for centuries, the current system was first adopted by meteorologists in the 1950s for naming hurricanes in the USA, following the realisation that using short names would make it easier to alert people to the risks and potential impacts. The World Meteorological Organization then began naming tropical cyclones and typhoons in the 1960s.

The UK Met Office and Republic of Ireland's Met Éireann adopted the system in 2015. Names are assigned when storms have the potential to cause amber or red wind warnings via the Met Office's National Severe Weather

Warnings service, or flooding and other major impacts arising from heavy rain or snow. For consistency, the naming conventions largely follow those used by the US National Hurricane Center in that storms are named in alphabetical order, alternating between male and female names, but omitting the letters Q, U, X, Y and Z. However, storms from another region retain their original name. For example, in 2020, ex-hurricane Epsilon hit our shores after being named by US weather forecasters, as did Storm Jorge, the remnants of a storm originally named in Spain.

The list is chosen by public consultation, with the selected names being published before the storm season begins in September, so if you'd like to get

ABOVE Sometimes a lee wave cloud forms in weak Helm conditions, similar in size and appearance to the Helm Bar but without the rotation.

RIGHT Dramatic cloudscapes during a Helm event.

OPPOSITE Cloud cloaking the hills during a Helm event.

OTHER NAMED WINDS OF THE WORLD

There is a certain romance about named winds, and some have permeated into our consciousness through films and literature. Even without knowing the details, there is a chance you may have heard of the fierce Mistral of southern France, the warm Santa Anas of the western USA, and the North African desert winds of Libya's Ghibli and Egypt's Khamsin. The Scirocco, Bora and Chinook have even inspired car and helicopter names. Almost 100 winds have been named worldwide, and their causes vary widely depending on the local climate and landscape.

Some, like the Helm, originate in hill and mountain areas that experience strong winds due to the local topography. These include the Mistral, whose cold blast is channelled along the Rhône valley, and the Bora of south and southeast Europe, which flows down to the Adriatic from the Dinaric Alps.

In contrast, some bring uncomfortably warm air with a risk of wildfires, such as the Santa Anas, which descend from desert mountains, accelerating as they are channelled along canyons towards the coast of southern California and northern Mexico. Further east, the Chinooks of the Rocky Mountains bring warm, dry air to the prairies of central USA, and are sometimes called 'snow eaters' due to their tendency to melt lying snow.

In flatter areas, named winds are more likely to be associated with local storms and depressions, as are the Ghibli and Khamsin. These sometimes generate huge sandstorms called haboobs as they cross the desert, blanketing towns and cities in dust. The Scirocco has similar causes but picks up moisture as it crosses the Mediterranean from North Africa, bringing hot, humid, windy weather to southern Europe.

BELOW A gigantic cloud of dust known as a haboob advances over Khartoum on 29 April 2007. These seasonal type of monsoons can reach a height of 914m (3,000ft) and can change the landscape in the few hours they last.
© Getty/STR/Stringer

In his remarkable book, *Where the Wild Winds Are*, author Nick Hunt set out on a quest to experience several named winds around Europe at first hand. The book describes his adventures together with many historical, cultural and scientific insights, including the following evocative passage:

The invisible alleyways of the air have twisted through mythology, in
and out of landscapes and cultures, from zephyrs to howling gales.
I have met the characters of the winds, and know the qualities they bring:
the Bora strength and clarity; the Foehn destruction and depression;
the Sirocco debilitation; the Mistral beauty and madness. Now it seems,
hoping against hope, I am about to know the Helm – if only the Bar will
come – and the wildness of the chase fills me, pulls me on.

involved in the next 'Name our Storms' exercise, watch for announcements on the Met Office's website. The UK Storm Centre website has more background on storm names and how they are selected.

The main benefit of storm forecasts is, of course, that they alert people to the risks of strong winds, flooding and other hazards. But weather enthusiasts often keep an eye out too for any interesting phenomena that may occur, such as the lightning displays and mammatus clouds described on page 79.

Even fog can have names

When warm, moist air passes over a cooler sea, it sometimes condenses into fog, often drifting inland on an onshore breeze. This is called sea fog and is prevalent enough on the east coast of Scotland to be known as a Haar. The online Merriam-Webster dictionary says that this was 'probably from a Low German or Dutch dialect word akin to Dutch dialect *harig* damp, misty, Middle Dutch *hare* sharp wind, piercing cold, Frisian *harig* misty, Old Norse *hārr* gray, hoary'.

The onshore breeze can either be part of the general weather circulation or due to a sea breeze, generated as warm air rising from coastal areas draws in cooler air from the sea. In summer this can spoil a day at the beach as fine weather gives way to misty, damp conditions. Roads and landmarks also become shrouded in mist so it is fair to say that most local residents do not see a Haar as something to celebrate!

Sea fog occurs in most coastal areas and is known as a 'sea fret' in northeast England. For the weather enthusiast, it can take on a rare charm if a well-defined front of mist approaches famous buildings, or is seen from on high. There are some great examples online from the Firth of Forth, including parts of Edinburgh rising from the mist.

Sea frets and Haar typically form between spring and autumn, particularly in early summer before the sea fully warms up. Sometimes they disperse with the heat of the day, but can persist if there is a consistent flow of moisture inland. For weather forecasters, sea fog is one of the most challenging phenomena to predict, as its formation and extent depends on several factors, including sea and land temperatures, humidity, and wind speed and direction.

However, local forecasters in Scotland and northeast England will often mention if a sea fret or Haar is expected. The cloud cover forecasts in the Met Office's UK Weather Map are another useful source of information – for example, sometimes showing tendrils of sea fog following valleys a long way inland later in the day.

OPPOSITE The Haar approaching a cruise ship moored in the Firth of Forth.

Tidal bore
Tidal race
Low tide walk

Pentland Firth

Falls of Lora

Corryvreckan/
Grey Dogs

Cramond Island

Lindisfarne

Nith Tidal Bore

St Mary's Island

Rough Island

Strangford Narrows

Arnside Bore

Morecambe Bay

Trent Aegir

Hilbre Island

The Swellies

Mersey Tidal Bore

Llanddwyn Island

Dee Tidal Bore

Wiggenhall Wave

The Bitches

Severn Bore

Worm's Head

Northey Island

The Broomway

Portland Race

St Michael's
Mount

Lihou Island

TIDES

CHAPTER 7

TIDAL BORES

See a line of surf passing woods and meadows far inland, and admire the power of the tide. Watch surfers attempt to ride the UK's largest tidal bore.

Highlights

◆
Marvel at a wall of water making its way up an estuary

◆
Admire the skill of surfers riding the UK's largest tidal bore

◆
See a river flow backwards on the incoming tide

What you might see

Tidal bores are spectacular surges that sweep inland on the highest tides, sometimes causing an impressive wave as they pass by. The UK's largest, the Severn Bore, is popular with surfers, with the longest ride exceeding several miles.

Water levels rise quickly after the tidal bore has passed, and the speed and power of the incoming flow can be most impressive to see. Some tidal bores travel many miles inland to reach places far from the sea, such as Chester, Gainsborough and Warrington.

Level of difficulty ★★★

LOCATION tidal bores occur in more than 20 estuaries around the UK
FREQUENCY varies from a few times a month to a few days a year
PREDICTABILITY in principle easy to predict, although with many sources of uncertainty
SAFETY normal outdoor risks, plus the risks from the tides

Level ★★★ for those featured in the text, Level ★★★★ to ★★★★★ for others around the UK

BELOW One of the UK's less well-known tidal bores on the Duddon Estuary in south Cumbria, seen against a backdrop of distant Lake District fells.

PREVIOUS PAGES An early morning view of the Trent Aegir in Nottinghamshire.

SPECTACULAR TIDES

On the highest tides, extraordinary surges sweep inland in more than 20 estuaries around the UK. These are called tidal bores and some reach heights of a metre or more. The largest and best known is the Severn Bore, famed as a place for surfers, kayakers and canoeists to test their skills on its extraordinary wave. Large crowds gather when a five-star event is predicted, and even helicopters sometimes follow the surge upstream, carrying news crews filming the spectacle. Other tidal bores occur from Somerset to southwest Scotland, and around the Wash and the Humber Estuary.

The first signs of a tidal bore usually appear near the coast. Here the gentle flow of water out to sea is disrupted by a line of surf ahead of the incoming tide. In its wake, sandbanks and mudflats quickly become submerged and channels merge to form an unbroken expanse of water. In calm weather you may even hear the roar of surf in the distance.

In the best conditions, the surge enters the narrower river channel further upstream to wind its way past fields and meadows, making a truly incongruous sight so far from the sea. Sometimes the cries of wading birds signal its approach as they are startled into flight. As the leading wave appears, the river flow seems to stop in its tracks before changing direction to head upstream.

Water levels rise quickly once the surge has passed, as what may have been tranquil water transforms into a strong current moving inland. If you are only used to seeing the tide at the coast, the speed of the flow can be most impressive to see.

Some tidal bores travel a long way inland, reaching towns and cities that you might not normally think of as affected by the tides. Examples include Bridgwater, Chester, Dumfries, Lancaster and Warrington. Of course, dig into their maritime past and some were major ports during the industrial

revolution. The town of Gainsborough is perhaps the furthest from the sea to be affected, and by boat is more than 100km (60 miles) from the mouth of the Humber Estuary.

The best times to see tidal bores are often in spring and autumn, when the highest tides of the year occur. However, some happen a few times a month all year, and timings are given below for popular examples. As with all natural phenomena, sightings are never guaranteed. There are many compensations if none appears, for example exploring the wide open vistas and wildlife of an estuary, or the delights of a riverside walk further inland.

WHY DO TIDAL BORES OCCUR?

Tidal bores form in estuaries with an unusually large difference between low and high tide – that is, a high tidal range. Normally, the tide comes in without much drama twice a day. Signs can include boats at anchor swinging through 180 degrees and ducks and gulls taking a free ride inland. Further upstream, river flows may reverse almost imperceptibly as the tide arrives, slowing to a halt before turning to head upstream. On calm days, the water surface may take on a choppy appearance as it is churned up by the tide.

However, on the highest tides, levels may rise so fast that a tidal bore forms. The rate of rise is typically greatest on the highest spring tides of the year, between February and April and August and October, or roughly when the clocks change to and from British Summer Time. Sightings are often possible in other months too, although the surge may be weaker or travel a shorter distance. Most start about two to three hours before high tide and take an hour or more to progress inland.

Tidal bores occur when the rising tide pushes huge amounts of water into an ever-narrowing channel, causing a surge to form. Estuaries come in many shapes and sizes, and the classical funnel shape starts as a narrow river channel and widens progressively towards the coast: the Arnside Bore and Nith Tidal Bore form in estuaries of this type. At the other extreme, some tidal bores occur in relatively narrow channels modified for shipping, such as the Trent Aegir and the Dee Tidal Bore.

Tidal bores are studied using the scientific discipline of hydraulics, which considers the motion of water and other fluids. At a given point, their characteristics depend on the water depth ahead of the surge and the speeds of the river flow and the incoming tide. Local complicating factors can include the shape of the channel, islands, bends, wind speed, wind direction, weirs, bridges and boat piers. However, river flows often have the greatest influence and some tidal bores may not form at all upstream if flows are high; the Lune Tidal Bore near Lancaster is a good example.

Two main types of tidal bores occur. So-called undular bores have a rounded leading edge, often followed by a train of smaller waves, which have

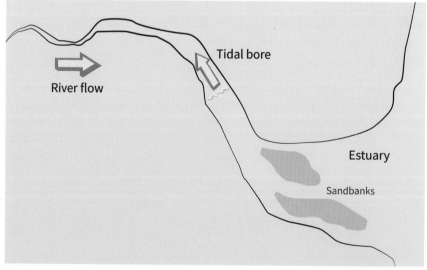

ABOVE Illustration of the passage of a tidal bore up a classical funnel-shaped estuary.

ABOVE A line of whelps follows a small tidal bore near Warrington in the Mersey Estuary.

the unusual name of whelps. By contrast, a breaking bore has a line of surf across some or all of its width, rather like waves breaking at a beach. A tidal bore can adopt both of these forms as it moves upstream, depending on local conditions.

MEDIEVAL TIDAL BORE WATCHING?

Tidal bores have long been known to river users and fishermen, who in some places appreciate the fish carried in on the incoming tide. However, there are few written accounts of observations before the birth of hydraulics as a scientific discipline. Perhaps the earliest known record is for the Wiggenhall Wave, which occurs near the village of Wiggenhall St Mary Magdalen in Norfolk. Tidal bore enthusiast Kevin Holland – who coined the name Wiggenhall Wave – has looked into its history and from a 1558 parish register found that:

'Wigrehale' was a Saxon name signifying 'a great force or press of water, both from the sea and River Ouse'. The word 'Wiggre', 'Wigre', 'Hygre' or 'Eagre' denoted a raging swell and 'Hale' meant all water. Hence, roughly translated, several hundred years ago the name of the village meant 'Land of the rushing waters'.

7. TIDAL BORES

THE SEVERN BORE

The best known tidal bore in the UK is the Severn Bore, which is also one of the most famous in the world. In the best conditions, its leading wave reaches heights of more than 2m (7ft) and speeds of more than 16km/h (10mph). It was the birthplace of tidal bore surfing, with the first attempt in 1955 by a former wartime commando leader, Colonel 'Mad Jack' Churchill. The record for a continuous ride stands at more than 12km (7.5 miles), held by surfing enthusiast Steve King.

The tidal influence in the River Severn normally begins at Maisemore Weir, close to Gloucester, although extends further upstream on the highest tides. In the upper reaches, the channel is flanked by woods and farmland, but by the town of Newnham-on-Severn it is more than a hundred metres wide, with extensive areas of sandbanks at low tide.

The Severn Bore is so powerful because the estuary has one of the highest tidal ranges in the world, exceeding 15m (49ft) on the highest tides. In the best conditions, the surge begins near the port of Sharpness and reaches Maisemore, where it comes to a sudden end on hitting the weir. The travel time is about two hours for the journey of about 32km (20 miles). However, sometimes it only forms in the estuarine or riverine parts of the estuary. Many factors affect its progress, and a useful guide from the Gloucester Harbour Trustees says:

Low pressure and SW winds can increase the size of the wave and speed it up making it arrive earlier. The reverse is true with high pressure and northerly winds. Fresh water levels affect the height of the wave significantly. Lots of rain can make the wave in the estuary end of the river, near Newnham, bigger. But it will then be too deep upstream to produce a wave. Conversely, low water levels can diminish the estuary wave but produce impressive clean faces upstream.

ABOVE Surfers await the arrival of the Severn Bore as dusk approaches, with a kayaker already riding the wave.

ABOVE The Wiggenhall Wave viewed on a fine, calm day.

Popular viewpoints include Newnham, Broadoak, Arlingham and Epney in the early stages, and Minsterworth, Stonebench, Over Bridge and Maisemore further upstream. The introduction to this book shows a photograph taken from Broadoak (see page 9). If you would like to celebrate after a sighting, popular spots include the Anchor Inn in Epney, the White Hart in Broadoak and the Severn Bore Inn near Minsterworth.

The best conditions are often said to be when the predicted high tide is

TIDAL BORES WORLDWIDE

Tidal bores occur on all continents except Antarctica, from the Amazon to Alaska and from Australia to Russia. The largest is the Qiantang Bore, which passes near Shanghai in China and is known as the Silver Dragon. It occurs more than 200 times a year, often reaching heights of several metres and speeds of 16–24km/h (10–15mph). Huge numbers of spectators gather for the largest events, particularly for the annual International Qiantang River Tidal Bore Watching Festival. Other countries in Asia that experience large tidal bores include India, Indonesia, Malaysia and Myanmar.

In France, the Seine Mascaret – or La Barre – was once a rival to the Qiantang Bore, reaching heights of several metres. However, nowadays it is much diminished due to river engineering works in the 1960s. The best known now are those on the Dordogne and Garonne rivers in southwest France.

In Canada, several tidal bores occur around the Bay of Fundy, which has the highest tidal range in the world. There is a well-established tourist industry linked to their passage, with waterside trails, viewing platforms and rafting adventure tours. Further west, an impressive tidal bore occurs in the Turnagain Arm of the Cook Inlet in Alaska. In Brazil, several tidal bores occur in the Amazon and its tributaries, where perhaps uniquely the main wave develops offshore before travelling into the wide river delta. Other locations include Australia, Mexico, Mozambique and Guinea-Bissau.

There are some great videos online of extreme surfers and kayakers riding the waves – challenges in the more exotic locations can include hypothermia, waterborne infections, water snakes, piranha and crocodiles.

Adapted from the author's publication *Tidal Bores of England, Scotland and Wales*

more than about 9.5m (31ft) at Sharpness, but the Severn Bore can form on lower tides too. The following two websites say more about the conditions for its formation and are well worth viewing before making a visit:

- The Severn Bore: a natural wonder of the world (severn-bore.co.uk)
- The Severn Bore: surfers and spectators (thesevernbore.co.uk)

The first includes a timetable showing when the best tidal bores are likely to occur and the second has a useful link to social media updates on the latest conditions. Both include a wealth of information about the history, characteristics, viewpoints and joys of the tidal bore. Traditionally, events are ranked on a scale of 1 to 5 stars, with 5 stars the best.

What's in a name?

While 'tidal bore' is perhaps the most common name for the surge along a river, the event goes by many other names around the world. In eastern England, tidal bores are often called *aegir* or *eagre*, a name thought to have Norse or Latin roots. The most famous example is the Trent Aegir. In France they are *mascaret*, meaning a steer (cow) with a mottled face. This arises from the Occitan language of southern France, and is inspired by the belief that a tidal bore resembles a herd of stampeding cattle. In Brazil a tidal bore is called a *pororoca*, which means 'great roar' in the indigenous Tupi language. This is both a general term specific to certain tidal bores that occur in the Amazon river. Other names in the English-speaking world include 'river tides', 'bore tides', 'bore waves' and 'tidal surges'.

Description adapted from the author's publication *Tidal Bores of England, Scotland and Wales*

A VIEWER'S GUIDE TO TIDAL BORES

Tidal bore prediction is not an exact science so, as with many other natural phenomena, it is best to travel in hope when trying to see one, but to have a backup plan in case conditions aren't quite right. The usual advice is to arrive well before high tide is predicted for a nearby site, such as a tide gauge or port. For example, for the Arnside Bore this might be at least two hours before high tide at Barrow-in-Furness. See pages 20–22 for tips on finding out tide times.

On arriving, the first thing to check is whether water is still flowing towards the coast, meaning that you haven't missed the tidal bore. On a windy day, waves can make the direction of flow surprisingly difficult to see,

so one tip is to watch rocks and debris on the shoreline to check they're not already being submerged by the tide.

However, if conditions aren't right, the flow may just change direction without any drama followed by the rapidly advancing tide, meaning you will need to try another time. It is worth waiting for the tide to turn though, since tidal bores sometimes pass later than expected.

A calm day provides the best viewing conditions as the wave stands out more relative to the water surface. Strong winds can break up the wave and even make it arrive much earlier than expected. Low river flows often help, although this is not a general rule. Given all these uncertainties, the website of the UK's National Tidal and Sea Level Facility (NTSLF) gives the following useful tips:

- *It is better to arrive half an hour too early than a minute too late – rainfall, wind and other factors affect the time of arrival of the bore; its appearance cannot be predicted with certainty.*
- *Bores can disappoint, because of various factors, even if the predicted tide is very high.*
- *If you can go a number of times you will have a better chance of seeing something quite awe inspiring.*

It is also important to watch out for your own safety, staying above high-water levels and not venturing out on to sandbanks, mudflats or saltmarshes. Once the surge has passed, levels rise surprisingly quickly, which regularly catches people out, sometimes resulting in a risky rescue. Parked cars can also be flooded. The Gloucester Harbour Trustees again provide the following useful advice for the Severn Bore, which is relevant to other tidal bores too:

> *People on the bank should be wary of standing too close to the edge of the bank. The wave can cause water levels to rise sharply as it passes and give the unwary a soaking or even knock them off their feet in extreme cases. The river levels can remain high for some time after the wave passes. Spectators and their vehicles have occasionally been cut off by rising waters necessitating rescue by the police. People should never be tempted to walk out on to exposed sandbanks as the surface is often soft and mud-like and they risk becoming stuck in quicksand as the wave approaches.*

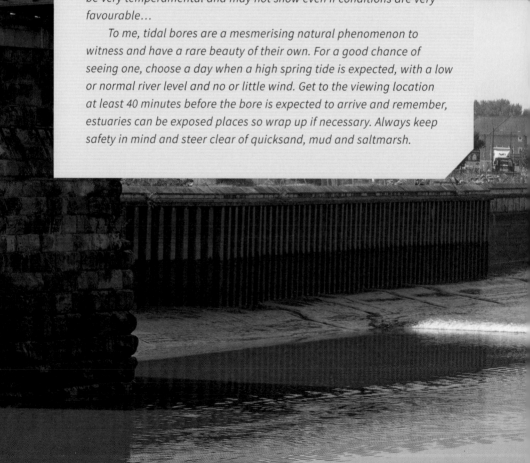

AN EXPERT'S VIEW

Tidal bore expert Rob Bridges has posted videos online for many of the UK's tidal bores and recalls some of his experiences:

The first tidal bore I witnessed was on the River Severn at Minsterworth. The bore was impressive; a 1.5m undular wave that smashed against the riverbanks. Knowing what I know now, I would have chosen a different location to get a better chance of seeing a more dramatic breaking wave.

In 2014, the River Dee hosted the most impressive bore I have seen. It was over one metre high and continually breaking as it approached Queensferry. Ironically this was the first bore I filmed and I have never seen one so spectacular since!

Getting to see some bores can prove trickier than others. For example, it took three visits to the River Douglas, a tributary of the River Ribble, before I had success. The bore only seems to appear on a short stretch of the river by the Marina. Other bores, such as on the Lune, can be very temperamental and may not show even if conditions are very favourable…

To me, tidal bores are a mesmerising natural phenomenon to witness and have a rare beauty of their own. For a good chance of seeing one, choose a day when a high spring tide is expected, with a low or normal river level and no or little wind. Get to the viewing location at least 40 minutes before the bore is expected to arrive and remember, estuaries can be exposed places so wrap up if necessary. Always keep safety in mind and steer clear of quicksand, mud and saltmarsh.

For the sake of local residents and future visitors, it is important to park cars sensibly and keep to public rights of way, closing gates along the way. More generally, there is a great tradition of supporting local businesses by visiting nearby pubs, cafés and shops, and some staff may have useful advice on when and where to see the local tidal bore.

For photographers, it is best to have your camera at the ready, since tidal bores sometimes appear when you least expect them. Fast shutter speeds help with capturing images of whelps and breaking waves. If you have a choice of viewpoints, look for a site with the sun behind you, and be aware of other possibilities as the surge goes past, such as spectacular flights of wading birds.

BELOW A kayaker rides the Lune Tidal Bore in Lancaster.

BEYOND THE SEVERN BORE

With more than 20 tidal bores around the UK, there is plenty of choice, but some are more difficult to spot than others. The table describes several in addition to the Severn Bore that are popular with spectators, although, as always, sightings aren't guaranteed. Additional sources of information on the UK's tidal bores appear in the Further reading section. The map at the start of this section also shows the locations of several more, including some that are much more challenging to see.

SIX POPULAR TIDAL BORES AROUND THE UK, BEYOND THE SEVERN BORE

Tidal Bore	Comments
Arnside Bore	The largest and best known of five tidal bores that occur in Cumbria. Due to the extreme risks from the tides, during the main tourist season the council sounds a siren twice a few minutes before the incoming tide, which as a side benefit gives advance warning of the approach of the tidal bore. The most popular viewpoints are along the promenade and pier in Arnside, where there is a good choice of pubs and cafés nearby. The website of the Arnside & Silverdale Area of Natural Beauty (AONB) includes tips on seeing the tidal bore along with other sights in this beautiful area.
Dee Tidal Bore	The largest tidal bore in Wales is unusual in that it is strongest where it passes through a straight-sided artificial channel called New Cut, which was built in the 18th century to improve navigation to Chester. Popular viewpoints include the embankment path around the Jubilee Bridge at Queensferry and the footbridge at Saltney Ferry. The website of the National Tidal and Sea Level Facility (NTSLF) has more background on the tidal bore and on when and where to see it.
Mersey Tidal Bore	The Mersey's tidal bore begins near Liverpool John Lennon airport and sometimes reaches Howley Weir in Warrington, a maximum distance of travel only exceeded by the Severn Bore and the Trent Aegir. Popular viewpoints include Wigg Island Community Park in Runcorn and the Forrest Way Bridge in Warrington, along with the waterside path near Wharf Street. Again, see the NTSLF website for information on timings.

Tidal Bore	Comments
Nith Tidal Bore	Scotland's largest tidal bore occurs in the Nith Estuary, and on the best days almost reaches The Caul in Dumfries, a beautiful weir near the town centre. Popular viewpoints include the pier at Glencaple, with a café and hotel nearby, and the waterside path at Kingholm Quay in the more riverine part of the estuary. The Caerlaverock Community Association website is an excellent source of information on the tidal bore and the many other sights in the area.
Trent Aegir	Widely considered to be the second largest tidal bore in the UK, the Trent Aegir starts in the River Trent shortly before it reaches the Humber Estuary and continues for about 40km (25 miles), past the historic town of Gainsborough. Popular viewpoints include the Chesterfield Canal area at West Stockwith and Riverside Walk in Gainsborough. Despite its height, the wave usually maintains a rounded undular form and only breaks occasionally. See the excellent web pages on the Crowle Community Forum website for more details.
Wiggenhall Wave	Also known locally as the *Eagre*, this is the only tidal bore that still occurs around the Wash, the others long gone due to historic works for navigation. The most accessible viewpoint is around the bridge across the Great Ouse in Wiggenhall St Mary Magdalen, although please park considerately to keep roads and driveways clear for local residents. The popular Cock Inn is nearby. Local enthusiast Kevin Holland suggests that the tidal bore is most likely to occur in spring and autumn when the tide at King's Lynn exceeds about 7m (23ft), and that the tide in Wiggenhall St Mary Magdalen changes about one hour before high tide in King's Lynn. There are several videos and news articles online that give more information about the wave, including attempts to surf it.

BELOW The Nith Tidal Bore approaching the pier at Glencaple.

CHAPTER 8

TIDAL RACES

Watch the spectacular waves and eddies caused when the tide races past islands and headlands, or into and out of lochs. See one of the world's largest tidal whirlpools.

Highlights

◆ Take a boat ride past a giant whirlpool

◆ Listen to the roar of the tides from a clifftop path

◆ Watch kayakers play at a loch outfall

What you might see

Spectacular waves sometimes occur when the tides are forced through a narrow gap, forming a tidal race. Some have earned themselves colourful names, such as The Bitches or The Merry Men of Mey. Submerged rocks can

also shed powerful eddies in their wake and even cause whirlpools to form, drawing water down into their depths.

The strongest tidal races are a challenge for the largest ships, while others are a playground for experienced kayakers and a rite of passage for yachting enthusiasts. For spectators, getting close enough to see them is part of the adventure, sometimes requiring a boat trip or a clifftop walk.

Level of difficulty ★★★

LOCATION some tidal races are in remote coastal areas
FREQUENCY often most impressive on the highest tides of the year
PREDICTABILITY can be affected by local currents, and wind speed and direction
SAFETY normal outdoor risks, and may involve boat trips or clifftop walks

The difficulty varies widely between individual tidal races; see text for details.

BELOW An early morning telephoto view of The Bitches, about an hour before high tide.

TIDAL SOUNDS

Tidal straits or sounds are one of the most common places to find tidal races. They usually occur where water is forced to flow quickly through a gap, but even slow currents can cause dangerous waters when they collide. Most are only accessible by boat, but landlubbers can head to Wales to view two spectacular tidal races: The Bitches and The Swellies.

The Bitches

The unusually named The Bitches are a line of jagged rocks that jut out from Ramsey Island into Ramsey Sound, some rising several metres above the waterline. The smaller rocks are called whelps, which interestingly share their name with the smaller waves behind some tidal bores.

The tidal race is also known as The Bitches, and is at its most powerful during spring tides, with standing waves, eddies and eddy lines forming downstream. Tidal currents can exceed several knots in the sound and are faster around the rocks. Even from land, in calm weather you can sometimes hear the sound of rushing water from several hundred metres away.

Local advice states that the best displays are usually about an hour before the peak of a high spring tide. To add to the danger, a small whirlpool sometimes forms above nearby Horse Rock, which rises more than 21m (69ft) from the seabed. Most kayaking guides strongly advise keeping well clear of this area, and the waters of The Bitches themselves are only for fully briefed experts.

From the mainland, a nearby headland provides the closest views, and lies on one of the finest sections of the Pembrokeshire Coast Path, near the picturesque harbour of St Justinian. The route is rocky and exposed in places, but with dramatic coastal views. Take binoculars for the best views.

St Justinian is also the base for wildlife boat tours to Ramsey Island and the more distant Skomer and Grassholm islands. Some trips pass the tidal race to spot dolphins or porpoises feeding in the churning waters, although check timings first to see if the tides are suitable. Other sightings can include gannets, seals and puffins. Tour boat operator websites are a good source of additional information on the tidal race and other places you might like to visit, including historic St Davids, Britain's smallest city.

The Swellies

Further north, The Swellies occur in the Menai Strait, and are strongest in the stretch between the two bridge crossings to Anglesey. These are the Britannia Bridge and the older Menai Suspension Bridge, a particularly impressive 19th-century structure designed by Thomas Telford.

The strait is less than 800m (0.5 miles) wide in this area, and as the tide is forced through the narrow gap, standing waves and eddies form. These are popular with expert kayakers when conditions are right. Several rock outcrops and small islands add to the challenge, including Swelly Rock from which the tidal race perhaps gets its name.

Due to the complex tides around Anglesey, there is often a marked difference in water levels between opposite ends of the strait. This further complicates flows, sometimes even causing opposing currents in part of the channel. Conditions are constantly changing over a tidal cycle but are usually most dramatic on a flood tide during spring tides. Although reports vary, you'll be more likely to see impressive waves when high tide at Holyhead is at least 5–6m (16–20ft).

The best views are from the wide scenic promenade between the Menai Bridge and Church Island (*Ynys Tysilio*). The island's 15th-century St Tysilio's Church makes for an interesting detour, and a war memorial atop a hill provides good views of the surrounding area. The island was once tidal and only accessible by a rocky low tide causeway, but a modern pedestrian causeway now only floods on extreme tides.

LOCH OUTFALLS

Loch outfalls are a more unusual place to find tidal races, and perhaps the most famous British examples occur in Scotland and Northern Ireland.

The Falls of Lora

In Scotland, the Falls of Lora occur just a few miles north of Oban, where Connel Bridge crosses the entrance to Loch Etive. Here the loch is just a couple

Britannia Bridge in the Menai Strait, with a weak tidal race in progress.

of hundred metres wide, and the flow is further restricted by a submerged rocky sill across part of the channel. Dramatic eddies and standing waves occur during the highest spring tides, making it a popular spot for experienced kayakers. On a falling (ebb) tide, there is sometimes an abrupt drop of a metre or more in water levels near the bridge, as it takes time for levels to equalise between the loch and the sea. As a nearby information panel says:

> At certain states of the tide you will see spectacular overfalls with a water level drop of up to 1.2m and a lot of white water in front of you. The Falls of Lora form at the shallow narrows where Loch Etive in the east meets the open sea of the Firth of Lorn in the west.

Currents of up to 12 knots have been observed. The falls occur on both the incoming (flood) and outgoing tide, with those on the ebb tide perhaps more spectacular. However, as with all tidal phenomena, they can be affected by wind and wave conditions. See the superb Falls of Lora website for more details (www.fallsoflora.info). Other places you might like to visit nearby include the historic town of Oban – also a popular departure point for boat trips further afield – and Loch Etive itself, which stretches more than 32km (20 miles) towards Glen Coe and is famed for its scenery and wildlife.

8. TIDAL RACES

WHAT IS A TIDAL RACE?

Tidal races usually form when a tidal flow is forced through a narrow gap, typically between an island and the mainland, or at the entrance to a loch. They are also found around headlands and peninsulas. What follows is some handy terminology, with thanks to the online dictionary of the International Hydrographic Organization for some definitions:

• **Eddy** – a circular movement of water usually formed where currents pass obstructions, between two adjacent currents flowing counter to each other, or along the edge of a permanent current.
• **Eddy line** – a line of eddies forming between two currents moving at different speeds, or even in different directions.
• **Overfall** – short, breaking waves occurring when a strong current passes over a shoal or other submarine obstruction or meets a contrary current or wind.
• **Standing wave** – a wave that remains roughly in one place relative to the seabed, typically forming downstream of a submerged obstacle, such as a reef or rock ledge.
• **Whirlpool** – a rotating area of water larger than an eddy, sometimes with an easily visible central core into which water descends.

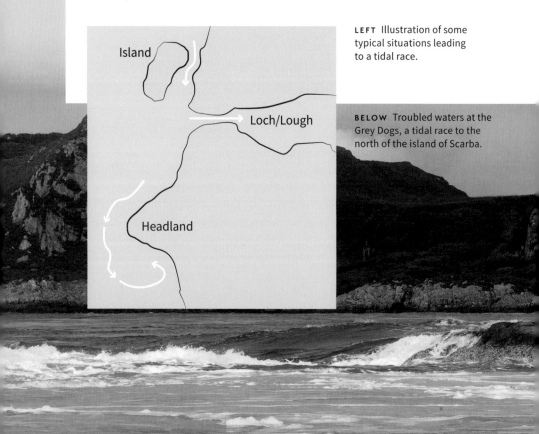

Island

Loch/Lough

Headland

LEFT Illustration of some typical situations leading to a tidal race.

BELOW Troubled waters at the Grey Dogs, a tidal race to the north of the island of Scarba.

Whirlpools have many similarities to eddies but differ in being larger and almost stationary relative to the seabed. Sometimes a noticeable dip of swirling water develops at the centre, similar to the flow at a plughole in a sink. An alternative name is maelstrom, a Scandinavian word of Dutch origin.

The fear of being drawn down into the depths has inspired many myths and legends, and whirlpools have also featured in fictional works. Perhaps the most famous are Edgar Allan Poe's *A Descent into the Maelstrom* and Jules Verne's *Twenty Thousand Leagues under the Sea*.

Tidal currents are usually at their strongest on a rising or falling spring tide. On navigation charts, they are often referred to as tidal streams, and their speed is usually expressed in knots, equal to one nautical mile per hour or about 1.85km/h (1.15mph). Sites with strong currents have great potential for tidal power generation, such as in the Pentland Firth, Strangford Narrows and Ramsey Sound.

Factors that can make a tidal race more violent include ocean swell and strong winds, particularly if the wind blows against the direction of the current. This wind-against-tide effect is well known to sailing and sea kayaking enthusiasts and can be a challenge to small craft.

In the absence of better information, a possible starting point for seeing tidal races is to arrive at roughly the half way point on a rising or falling spring tide: that is, two to three hours before or after the peak. On subsequent visits, refine the timings based on past experience. See pages 20–22 for tips on tidal safety and more background on the terminology used.

ABOVE Expert kayakers tackle the Falls of Lora on an ebb tide.

Strangford Lough

Northern Ireland has its share of challenging tidal races, particularly along the north coast around Rathlin Island. However, the best known is in the entrance to Strangford Lough, along a channel known as The Narrows. Here the strait is less than half a mile wide, with many submerged rocks and outcrops. On the highest tides, this sometimes causes eddies, standing waves and even a small whirlpool, known as the Routen Wheel. On an ebb tide, conditions near the entrance to the Narrows can be particularly dangerous to small craft when there is a strong onshore wind, causing violent waves up to 3.2km (2 miles) offshore.

Spotting these phenomena from land is a challenge, although with luck you might see signs near two navigation aids in the channel: the Salt Rock Beacon and the Gowland Marker. In the right conditions, you can also get a feel for the strength of the flows from the waterfronts at nearby Portaferry and Strangford. However, rather than searching for outfalls, most people visit the area for the fabulous scenery, wildlife and historic sites, which include a walk to a low tide island and huge numbers of brent geese, as described in later chapters.

BRITAIN'S LARGEST WHIRLPOOL

South of Oban, another spectacular sight awaits: the Corryvreckan Whirlpool. This is reputed to be the third largest in the world and forms in the Gulf of Corryvreckan between the island of Jura and its smaller neighbour, Scarba. Flows here are so violent because, as the tides ebb and flow, water levels to the west differ from those in the more constricted area between the mainland and the islands. In some conditions, this causes water to rush through the gulf, where a submerged basalt buttress known as the Old Hag imparts a spin, causing the whirlpool. The buttress is just one of several that jut out from a submerged cliff running roughly parallel to the Scarba shore, causing turbulent waters through much of the strait. These effects, particularly during a flood tide, are accentuated by a strong westerly wind blowing along the gulf.

There are many stories and legends associated with the whirlpool, including a disputed tale that the Royal Navy once deemed the strait to be unnavigable. Remarkably, the author George Orwell had to be rescued nearby after a family boat trip into the gulf nearly turned to disaster. At the time, he had just started work on his book *1984*, while staying in a remote farmhouse on Jura.

Some legends suggest that the whirlpool is named after a Scandinavian Prince, Breackan, who was asked to prove his suitability to marry a local princess in a boat handling challenge in the gulf. Another version of the tale presents him as a bloodthirsty raider, with the whirlpool conjured up by the Old Hag to entrap him and his troops. More prosaically, the whirlpool's name may derive from a combination of the Gaelic words for cauldron and for speckled or chequered, relating to the appearance of the waves.

Most people visit the whirlpool by boat and several companies operate trips to the area. A visit can be truly dramatic due to the height of the waves, the strength of the current and the number of eddies. Departure points include Easdale, Port Askaig and Crinan: check operators' websites to see which departure times give the most favourable tides for a sighting. Some trips visit the Grey Dogs tidal race too, and many feature the fabulous wildlife in the area, which can include dolphins, basking sharks, sea eagles and seals. From land, the gulf can be seen from the northern end of Jura, but this would be a long hike from the nearest road.

ABOVE Rough conditions in the Gulf of Corryvreckan, with the hint of a large eddy or whirlpool; the whirlpool is sometimes better defined than on this day.

BELOW The Corryvreckan Whirlpool. © Geograph/ Walter Baxter

HEADLANDS AND PENINSULAS

Violent seas can also occur as the tides ebb and flow past headlands and peninsulas, sometimes causing problems even for large vessels. Examples include Hartland Point in Devon, the Lizard in Cornwall and the Mull of Kintyre in Scotland. In England, perhaps the most feared is Portland Race near Weymouth. This occurs off the tip of the Isle of Portland, a spectacular tied island (peninsula) that juts out into the English Channel.

The Portland Race occurs as the tide ebbs and flows past the peninsula, causing huge rotating areas of water to form downstream, at times several miles across. This causes currents to flow southwards along both sides of the peninsula, meeting dramatically near the tip, where they collide with the wider flow. Conditions are further complicated by a submerged rock shelf that extends more than a mile offshore, known as Portland Ledge, and a sandbank further offshore called The Shambles.

The widely varying currents often produce large, steep waves heading in random directions, particularly on a windy day. Due to the complexity of the flows, it is difficult to give any definitive guidelines on when to visit, although spring tides are likely to be best. Gales and storms are best avoided due to the possibility of powerful waves. Small craft usually give these waters a wide berth.

From land, the tidal race is best seen from Portland Bill at the tip of the peninsula. This is a popular area for coastal walking and many visitors take a trip up the lighthouse. If you have time, on first reaching the Isle of Portland it is worth stopping for the fabulous view of Chesil Beach, an almost 32km (20-mile) long shingle beach that runs parallel to the Dorset shoreline, itself a natural wonder.

SOME RECORD-BREAKING TIDAL RACES

With so many factors affecting tidal races, several compete for the title of the most powerful in the world. The fastest is often said to be the Saltstraumen Maelstrom in Norway, which occurs at the entrance to the Skjerstad Fjord, just inside the Arctic Circle. The loch entrance is about 150m (500ft) wide at this point and sights include strong currents, violent waves and eddies.

There is more competition for the title of the strongest whirlpool. The Moskenstraumen in the Lofoten islands in Norway tops many lists, and is often simply called the Maelstrom. Another contender is the Old Sow near the US/Canada border, which often places in second place and occurs near the mouth of the Bay of Fundy. Its name is sometimes said to derive from the sucking and squealing sound it makes at its peak, resembling that of a pig, or less interestingly from *sough*, meaning a type of drain. The bay has the largest tidal range in the world, exceeding 16m (52ft) on the highest tides.

Some of the most feared seas at a strait are in the Pentland Firth in Scotland. The narrow straits here generate fierce eddies, whirlpools and steep chaotic waves as the tides rise and fall. In places, tidal streams can reach 16 knots, often said to be the fastest in the British Isles. Some of its tidal races have names, of which the most famous is The Merry Men of Mey.

Further north, Sumburgh Roost is one of the best known tidal races in the Shetland Isles, and sometimes extends several miles from Sumburgh Head towards Fair Isle. Roust (also *roost, rust, rost, roast*) is a Gaelic word that the Scottish National Dictionary defines as 'a turbulent stretch of sea caused by a strong current in a restricted passage or by the meeting of conflicting currents'. Many more tidal races are known to seafarers and appear on the navigation charts used by yachting enthusiasts, sea kayakers and commercial vessel operators. The *Reeds PBO Small Craft Almanac* is a popular source of information.

OPPOSITE The lighthouse at Portland Bill, with a choppy sea beyond, on a day with a moderate wind. The sea is much rougher in storm conditions.

CHAPTER 9

LOW TIDE WALKS

Walk across the seabed to a tidal island to explore rockpools and historic ruins. Take a guided walk across Morecambe Bay with the King's Guide to the Sands.

Highlights

◆
Explore the medieval
ruins on a holy island

◆
Visit wild, scenic
islands without a boat

◆
Walk with the King's
Guide to the Sands

What you might see

There is something magical about walking to an island along a route only recently beneath the sea. Some paths follow a well-marked causeway, but others wind their way across mud, rocks and sand. Crossing an estuary or bay from shore to shore gives a similar sense of achievement,

sometimes following ancient routes that are submerged twice a day.

These trips can make a beautiful day out following the still receding tide, and island sights can include castles, nature reserves, lighthouses, seals or just the pleasure of a remote beach away from it all. All the while, of course, keeping an eye on the time to be sure you head back well before the tide returns.

| Level of difficulty | ★★★ |

LOCATION tidal islands are only found in some coastal regions
FREQUENCY some routes are rarely accessible or require a guide
PREDICTABILITY great care is needed to check tide times and the weather forecast
SAFETY normal outdoor risks, plus significant risks from the tides, storms and quicksand

The difficulty varies widely between individual routes; see the text for details.

BELOW St Mary's Lighthouse near Whitley Bay.

ABOVE A refuge box (an elevated wooden platform or shelter) along the Pilgrim's Way to Lindisfarne.

HOLY ISLANDS

As Christianity spread in the Middle Ages, islands became important as a place for retreat, their remoteness helping with contemplation. Some sites were on tidal islands and their ruins make fascinating places to visit today.

Lindisfarne

One of the most famous was Lindisfarne in northeast England, also known as Holy Island. Here, St Aidan became the first settler on founding a monastery in the 7th century, invited by King Oswald of Northumbria to relocate from Iona, the cradle of Christianity in Scotland. Although the monastery is long gone, the ruins of the much grander 12th-century Lindisfarne Priory remain, having fallen into disrepair after the dissolution of the monasteries by Henry VIII. Some of its stonework was used to build the 16th-century Lindisfarne Castle, perched dramatically on a rock outcrop.

At about 5km (3 miles) long, Lindisfarne is one of Britain's largest tidal islands, and you can find a choice of cafés, pubs, shops and accommodation. For wildlife lovers, its surrounding dunes, saltmarsh and mudflats form part of a national nature reserve known for seals and wading birds.

Most visitors arrive by car or bus along the causeway road.

TIDES

Northumberland County Council publishes safe crossing times and suggests that you allow extra time in case the tide comes in early. Despite this, drivers still occasionally have to seek the safety of a refuge box after abandoning their cars to the sea – an expensive mistake. The National Trust and English Heritage recommend booking tickets ahead for the castle and priory.

St Michael's Mount

More than 500 miles south, the rocky island of St Michael's Mount in Cornwall is another historic holy place. Access is along a cobbled causeway, and in the tourist season there is a ferry to the island's picturesque harbour.

Beyond the visitor centre, a steep path rises through wooded slopes to the medieval castle that crowns the island, with great coastal views along the way. On a misty day, you can easily imagine monks walking this route. Lower down, the walled garden houses a variety of rare plants that thrive in the mild climate. The island is managed jointly by the St Aubyn family and the National Trust, and tickets for the castle and/or gardens must be booked in advance via the Trust's website.

Lihou Island

Further south, the ruins of 12th-century Lihou Priory lie on Lihou Island, a tidal island off the coast of Guernsey. From nearby L'Eree Headland, a more ominous relic overlooks the causeway – a former naval observation tower, serving as a reminder that the Channel Islands were the only part of the UK to be occupied during the Second World War.

THE PILGRIM'S WAY TO LINDISFARNE

Before the causeway was opened in the 1950s, the main access to Lindisfarne was via a traditional route called the Pilgrim's Way. This can still be walked today and is marked by a line of posts across the sands. It is a chance to follow in the steps of saints, monks and pilgrims, and appreciate the risks that were taken many centuries ago.

Normally there is only time to walk the route one way. The Northumberland County Council website provides key advice on the crossing, including that it should only be attempted with someone who has local knowledge. However, perhaps the safest way of all is with a professional guide, and the Northumberland Coast AONB website provides links to companies that run guided walks along the route.

The island is now a haven for wildflowers, wading birds and intertidal marine life, such as crabs and shellfish. The only habitation is Lihou House, a self-catering hostel primarily for school and youth groups. The causeway is eroded in places, with some tricky terrain for the less sure of foot, although with the pleasure of rock pools to explore along the way. You will need one to two hours to walk around the island, with great views inland and of the jagged rocks offshore, the rolling lines of surf attesting to the danger of these waters.

Safe crossing times are displayed on a noticeboard near the start of the walk, or can be obtained from the Visitor Information Centre in St Peter Port and the States of Guernsey website. The island is a good example of one where the tides only fall low enough on some days, so is not accessible on every day of the month.

GETTING AWAY FROM IT ALL

Another joy of tidal islands is the chance to walk to a remote coastal area with spectacular views inland. Two islands in Wales and one in Scotland provide splendid and very different examples of this experience.

Worm's Head

The unusually named Worm's Head (*Ynys Weryn*) lies close to the beautiful sands of Rhossili Bay on the Gower Peninsula near Swansea. The island stretches in a long line out from the shore, its rocky silhouette ending at a blunt-topped peak reminiscent of the head of a worm or serpent, hence the

ABOVE The causeway at Lihou Island starting to appear in the distance as the tide falls.

name. From the National Trust car park near the village of Rhossili, the coastal path leads down past exposed clifftops to a Coastwatch lookout station, where volunteers watch for people in danger. Crossing times are posted in the window at the station and safety information is posted on the National Coastwatch Institution website. An information board near the start of the path says whether the island is open or closed; if in doubt do not proceed!

If you are not used to hillwalking, the crossing can be challenging, with uneven and jagged rocks requiring a steadying hand in places, particularly at the start. On the island, the path leads to Inner Head, which is worth climbing for the superb coastal views. For the more sure-footed, it then continues to the head of the serpent, requiring more rock scrambling and crossing a natural rock bridge with some steep drops alongside; watch out for any nesting bird restrictions. The less well-known tidal island of Burry Holms lies at the other end of Rhossili Bay.

Llanddwyn Island

Further north, Llanddwyn Island (*Ynys Llanddwyn*) provides an equally spectacular but gentler introduction to low tide walks. The route crosses a wide expanse of sand, with wonderful distant views of Snowdonia on a fine day. The usual route starts from the main beach car park in Newborough Forest, from where you can walk along the shoreline or follow a woodland path to reach the wide area of sand that leads to the island. The longer Saint, Sand and Sea trail includes the island too. Information boards at the car park warn of the risk from high tides and the need to check tide times before

ABOVE Walkers heading along the beach towards Llanddwyn Island.

setting off. Dog walkers should also check if any seasonal restrictions apply.

Picturesque Tŵr Mawr lighthouse lies near the far end of the island –
its squat shape is thought to be modelled on the windmills once common
on Anglesey. Seals sometimes bask on the small rocky islands nearby.
Several information boards along the way describe the local geology, history
and wildlife, with one noting that Llanddwyn means 'the church of Saint
Dwynwen' and that 'St Dwynwen, patron saint of lovers of Wales, is connected
with this island where she lived in a convent and a church was established in
her name during the 5th century'.

Cramond Island

For a more urban experience, Cramond Island lies in the northwest of
Edinburgh, near the village of Cramond. Its causeway is nearly a mile long,
with fine views back to the city and along the Firth of Forth, including its
famous road and rail bridges. The island is uninhabited and the only buildings
are relics from the Second World War. It is popular with local residents and
tourists, and birdwatchers who visit to see wading birds at the shoreline and
woodland birds inland.

Safe crossing times are displayed at the start of the causeway and appear
on the RNLI's website. You can also obtain them by texting CRAMOND to
81400; call charges may apply. The route is mainly along concrete and stone
but can be slippery at times, with a few steep steps to negotiate near the start.
Photographs of the route at low and high tide appear in the introduction to
this book on pages 22 and 23.

WILDLIFE ISLANDS

In addition to coastal scenery, some tidal islands are best known for their wildlife, including seals and wading birds.

Northey Island

In Essex, Northey Island is famed for the many waterbirds that arrive in autumn and winter. These include redshank, brent geese and black tailed godwit. In recent years, work has been underway to regenerate saltmarsh around the island, a great habitat for fish, birds and plants.

The normal route to the causeway is from the Promenade Park car park in Maldon. A path runs part way around the island allowing you to take in the estuary views, including its many yachts and the occasional barge. The island is owned by the National Trust and access is seasonal and by permit only – obtained by sending an email to the address shown on the Trust's website. The return email includes information on crossing times and the route to the island.

Hilbre Island

Further north, Hilbre Island is the largest of a chain of three tidal islands off the northwestern tip of the Wirral peninsula. On a clear day, you can see all the way from the Port of Liverpool to north Wales across the mouth of the Dee Estuary. In summer, Atlantic grey seals sometimes swim near the picturesque remains of a lifeboat station, poking their heads above the water to watch the antics of visitors onshore. Dramatic sandstone rock formations add to the interest. The Dee Estuary is one of the UK's top birdwatching sites and the islands are a well-known high tide roost for wading birds.

The Friends of Hilbre Island website describes the safe walking route. This is via Little Eye, the smallest of the three islands, and due to deep water and quicksand the direct route must never be attempted. The walk starts from the Dee Lane slipway next to the Marine Lake at West Kirby where an information board gives more essential information on the route and tide times.

St Mary's Island

In Tyne and Wear, St Mary's Island is another fascinating place to visit, close to the seaside town of Whitley Bay. Tide times appear on the North Tyneside Council website and information boards near the start of its short causeway. The impressive lighthouse is climbed by 137 steps. The rocky shores beyond are part of a local nature reserve, which from autumn to spring is a renowned site for wading birds. Wander round to the back of the lighthouse and cottages and with luck you may see seals basking on the rocks and foreshore.

ABOVE View of Little Eye from West Kirby, with the Point of Ayr Lighthouse and hills of north Wales in the distance.

BELOW Rough Island at Strangford Lough in Northern Ireland is another great wildlife destination, where you can see large flocks of brent geese and wading birds at certain times of year. You can reach it around low tide; signs near the start of the causeway give details.

WHAT IS A TIDAL ISLAND?

As the tides fall, numerous rocky outcrops and sandbars appear around the coastline, some of which might be counted as tidal islands. However, in his book *No Boat Required: Exploring Tidal Islands*, author Peter Caton suggests that to qualify as tidal an island should be:

> *A named area of land of significant size, which supports vegetation, shows signs of human activity, can be safely walked to with dry feet at least once a month from the UK mainland, and is totally surrounded by water on a minimum of one tide each month, but never totally submerged.*

Using this definition, he identified 43 tidal islands around the coast of the UK and the book describes his adventures and misadventures visiting them all. Almost half were in Scotland, with the rest in England and Wales.

Challenges he described included: 'lost bus drivers, disappearing footpaths, precipitous cliffs, glutinous mud, hostile island owners, or the sea and its tides', while highlights included 'semi tropical gardens nestled under the castle on St Michael's Mount, the expanse of Rhossili Bay with tidal islands at each end' and 'the guided walk across Morecambe Bay to Chapel Island'.

However, some required a return visit, such as Hestan Island in the

Solway Firth, as 'walking in a remote place, with freezing weather and possibly quicksands that could have appeared since the last person crossed to Hestan was just too risky. I didn't want to be featured on the front page of Auchencairn News, pictured with a bearded Mountain Rescue man in a woolly jumper under the headline "Bloody idiot!"'

As he continues: 'It is essential that one has information on tide times, safe crossing periods and routes. The only safe way to visit a few of the islands is with a guide... Remember that the islands are beautiful places, but the sea, mud and cliffs are all potential killers.'

TIDAL ISLANDS AROUND THE WORLD

Tidal islands are found around the world and it is not just in Britain that people enjoy the challenge and beauty of a visit. Perhaps the most famous is Mont Saint Michel in Normandy in France, topped by a dramatic 11th-century abbey. In medieval times, the monks here oversaw religious activities at both St Michael's Mount in Cornwall and Lihou Island in Guernsey. Nowadays most visitors arrive by a road bridge opened in 2014, but tourist trips are still run across the sands.

The longest low tide crossing is probably that between Jindo and Modo islands in South Korea. This follows a natural causeway almost 3.2km (2 miles) long. A local festival dubbed the Moses Miracle is held twice a year and thousands of people make the journey.

The highest tides in the world occur in the Bay of Fundy in Canada. Tourist activities linked to the tides include so-called ocean floor walks at Burncoat Head, where vast areas of sand are exposed at low tide.

Risks and rewards: safety concerns

The low tide walks in this chapter were chosen because there is readily available information online and/or at the destination on routes, safety and crossing times. These range from walks that are possible on most days through to some that are only accessible at certain times of the year due to the tides or the need for a guide.

However, there are still risks, the most obvious being the tides. High tide is normally reached twice a day, but most routes are submerged long before this and some are only passable for an hour or two around low tide. Low (neap) tides themselves vary on both a fortnightly and seasonal basis so the time available varies throughout the year.

As tidal prediction is not an exact science, you need to leave plenty of spare time for your return. Days with strong winds and large waves must be avoided, as the tide can rush in sooner than expected, particularly if it is stormy at sea. It is therefore important to always check the weather and sunset times before setting off, including that fog is not forecast. Other potential risks include areas of soft mud and quicksand, a soupy mix of sand and water that can set around your legs like concrete. If in any doubt, leave the trip for another day.

Even on some of the easiest routes, the RNLI and Coastguard are regularly called out due to people misunderstanding or ignoring advice. And if you do get caught out by the tides, it is essential to stay ashore and not try wading or swimming, since the water usually rushes in much more quickly than at a beach (see pages 20–22 for more on this).

Particularly in more remote areas, it is advisable to take a fully charged phone and contact details for emergencies along with a map, waterproofs, spare food, water and warm clothing, much as you would if going hillwalking. Some routes cross slippery mud or jagged seaweed-covered rocks still wet after being submerged, so you will need stout footwear that you don't mind getting wet and a change of shoes for the trip home.

Despite all these risks, don't be put off because a fantastic day out awaits if you follow the relevant advice. Several more challenging walks are mentioned, but you would need to do your own research and gain some experience first. Risks on more advanced crossings include that the island may only be accessible on rare occasions, that navigation may be a problem due to featureless terrain, that the safe time for a crossing is unusually short, and that the going underfoot may be potentially dangerous.

CROSS BAY ROUTES

Before the days of road and rail, low tide routes provided a shortcut across estuaries, helping travellers to avoid a longer journey by land on poor paths or roads. Examples included Hale Ford across the Mersey Estuary near Liverpool, and the so-called 'waths' across the Solway Firth between Scotland and England, which date back to at least Roman times.

The Guide to the Sands

Perhaps the most famous and dangerous crossing is across Morecambe Bay, where the tides are said to come in faster than a galloping horse. Due to the risks, travellers would traditionally follow a route across the Kent and Leven estuaries marked out by the 'Guide to the Sands'. This post was first established in medieval times by the monks of Furness, Cartmel and

Conishead priories, and the Guide had to survey the route every day due to the frequently moving sands. For about 70 years there was even a scheduled horse-drawn stagecoach service between Lancaster and Ulverston, its timetable changing daily with the tides.

This tradition continues today in the form of guided Cross Bay Walks across the Kent Estuary with the King's Guide to the Sands. The walks have raised millions of pounds for charity and provide a fabulous day out, giving you the chance to make this risky crossing, which would be foolhardy to attempt alone. Taking several hours, surprises include the ever-changing Lake District views and just how far out into Morecambe Bay you travel.

At the main river channel, the Guide leads everyone across together, through water that is often knee or even waist deep. Tractors are on hand in case anyone needs a lift during the walk and, following tradition, the route is still marked out in advance with branches of laurel, skirting areas of deep water and quicksand. Charity walks are also run occasionally to Chapel Island, a historic island far out in the Leven Estuary and famed for its birdlife.

Since 1877 the guides have been appointed by the Guide over Sands Trust, a charity set up by the Duchy of Lancaster. The current post holders are Michael Wilson and Raymond Porter for the Kent and Leven portions of the route. Michael is a local fisherman and still ventures out on to the sands in between bay walks, musseling, shrimping, cockling, net fishing and boat fishing. Raymond is also an active fisherman. Michael's predecessor was Cedric Robinson MBE, who held the post for more than 50 years and wrote several fascinating books on Morecambe Bay and the celebrities and VIPs he guided across the sands. The Trust's website lists walk dates, which typically run between spring and autumn.

THE DEADLIEST PATH IN BRITAIN

Of all the low tide walks in Britain, one of the most extreme is along the Broomway, which crosses Maplin Sands to Foulness Island in Essex. For centuries, the Broomway was the main way to reach the island, until a bridge was built in the 1920s to serve a Ministry of Defence firing range and research centre, so it is normally closed to the public. In addition to tidal dangers, walkers run the risk of straying into quicksand or getting lost in mist or fog on this featureless terrain. Professional mountain leader Tom Bennett has run guided walks to the island for several years and says of the walk:

> The Broomway is an outer-worldly public right-of-way path nestled in the mouth of the Thames Estuary. Its large, shallow pools of sea water can mirror the sky causing the horizon line to disappear, the distant container ships left levitating in their place. But despite its wonder and beauty, the Broomway has claimed the lives of many men, women and children who have misjudged a crossing over the last six centuries, giving it its notoriety as the 'Deadliest Path in Britain'.

BELOW The featureless expanse of Maplin Sands at sunset under a full moon. The start of the Broomway lies a few hundred metres to the left of this point.

LAND

Legend:
- Rutting deer
- Autumn colours
- Wildflower displays
- *(s) snowdrops*
- *(b) bluebells*
- *(c) cherry blossoms*

Glen Affric
Urquhart Bay Wood *(b)*
Highland Wildlife Park
Queen's View
Big Tree Country
Birks of Aberfeldy
Cambo Estate *(s)*
Glen Finglas *(b)*
Kilmun
Pittencrieff Park *(c)*
Beecraigs Country Park
Royal Botanic Garden
The Meadows *(c)*

The Dark Hedges
Prehen Wood *(b)*
Glenariff
Wallington Hall *(s)*
Killaloo Wood *(b)*
Kielder Forest
Borrowdale
Springhill *(s)*
Ennerdale
Martindale
The Argory *(s)*
Muncaster Castle *(b)*
Thorp Perrow
Gosford Forest Park
Thirlmere
Roseberry Topping *(b)*
Castle Ward *(b)*
Tarn Hows
Castlewellan
Grizedale
Studley Royal
Forest *(b)*
Fountains Abbey *(s)*
Sizergh Castle *(c)*
The Stray *(c)*
Rivington
Dunham
Massey *(s)*
Bodnant Garden *(s)*
Tatton
Clumber Park *(b)*
Penrhyn Castle *(s)*
Park *(c)*
Sherwood Forest
Holkham Hall
Plas Power Woods
Rode Hall *(s)*
Blickling Estate *(b)*
Chirk Castle *(b, s)*
Bodenham
Easton Walled Gardens *(s)*
Arboretum
Anglesey
Painswick *(s)*
Colesbourne Gardens *(s)*
Abbey *(s)*
Dinefwr
Batsford Arboretum *(c)*
RSPB
Coed Cefn *(b)*
Stowe *(s)*
Minsmere
National Botanic Garden
Blenheim Palace
Forest of Dean
Richmond Park
Newark Park *(s)*
Cliveden *(b)*
Kew Gardens *(c)*
Westonbirt Arboretum
Welford
Knole Park
Exmoor
Park *(s)*
Brogdale Farm *(c)*
Stourhead
Sissinghurst Castle *(b)*
Hartland Abbey *(b)*
Winkworth
Bedgebury Forest
Arboretum
Kingston Lacy *(c,s)*
Sheffield Park *(b)*
New Forest
Buckland Abbey *(b)*
RSPB Arne
Godolphin *(b)*

CHAPTER 10

AUTUMN COLOURS

*Visit some interesting and unusual places, such as
Atlantic rainforests, to see autumn colours. See ancient trees
that have been around for hundreds of years.*

Highlights

◆
Admire an Atlantic
rainforest in its autumn
colours

◆
Get a flavour of the
fall colours of New
England and Japan

◆
Wonder at trees
that were around in
medieval times

What you might see

As the nights draw in, many trees burst into glorious autumnal colours before their leaves fall for the winter. This is one of the easiest natural spectacles to see, occurring in towns, cities and woods throughout the British Isles.

However, it is worth travelling for the most spectacular displays, such as in historic forests or against a backdrop of famous landmarks or ancient trees. Exotic imported trees can also produce intense displays at country parks and arboretums.

Level of difficulty

LOCATION can be seen in most places
FREQUENCY typically in autumn and early winter
PREDICTABILITY timing depends on recent weather conditions
SAFETY the normal risks of outdoor activities

The timing and intensity of autumn colours vary from year to year.

OPPOSITE Fiery displays can also be seen in some city centres, as in this example looking across the Water of Leith in Edinburgh.

PREVIOUS PAGES The Ennerdale Valley in the Lake District is the site of Wild Ennerdale, one of the UK's oldest and most successful rewilding projects, where activities include replacing conifers with broadleaf trees and allowing the River Liza (shown) to follow a more natural course.

AUTUMNAL CHANGES

Trees contribute to our well-being in many ways, brightening the dullest landscape and providing shade in hot weather. In spring, many burst forth with blossom, attracting bees and butterflies, while later in the year birds and mammals feed on their nuts and fruits.

It is in autumn, though, that the most spectacular changes occur when deciduous trees gain an array of colours, including golden yellows, rich oranges and fiery reds, before the leaves eventually drop, helping the trees to conserve energy and moisture during the winter and reducing the risk of frost and wind damage.

The first signs of change usually appear in the north at higher elevations, reaching lowland areas in southern England within the next month. The timing depends on the species – for example, the golden colours of beech sometimes appear in late August, but some oaks may not reach their full display until October. In many places the show is over by mid-November,

although it sometimes continues into December. Woodland colours last longer if there are several species, each reaching its best coloration in turn.

The colours are weather dependent. One factor leading to a good display seems to be a sunny summer with normal rainfall, followed by a run of cool, dry, frost-free days into autumn. Soil moisture variations may also cause individual trees to shed their leaves at different times, particularly in hilly areas. A very dry spring and summer or autumn storms may cause leaves to drop earlier than usual.

There are many great places where you can see autumn colours. For trees in their natural setting, woods and forests provide a great day out, while the more managed grounds of historic parks and country estates often have the added bonus of a property with a café to visit. The sites in this chapter have been chosen because of their historical significance or regular appearances in newspaper or magazine 'best of' or 'top ten' listings. Local enthusiasts, friends and colleagues can probably suggest more.

BELOW Autumn colours at Queen's View in Perthshire, which looks out over Loch Tummel. Queen Victoria visited this viewpoint in 1866, but local information boards suggest that it was probably named after Isabella of Mar, the first wife of Robert the Bruce. It is a popular spot to visit, with a shop, information room and café nearby.

WHEN TO SEE AUTUMN COLOURS

Of all the natural spectacles in this book, autumn colours are probably the easiest to see. However, you can still have a wasted journey through arriving too early in the year or after leaves have fallen in an autumn storm. For local sites, simply keeping an eye on nearby trees may be enough to decide when best to visit. If travelling further, it's worth searching destination names and the #autumnwatch hashtag on social media. Keep an eye out too for local news stories and blog posts from the Woodland Trust, the National Trust, the National Trust for Scotland, Forestry England, Forestry and Land Scotland, and Natural Resources Wales. The websites of these organisations are also a great place to look for more ideas for places to visit.

With Britain's changeable weather, a visit can be chilly even in early autumn, when the nights start drawing in. You should therefore take warm clothing and a torch, along with suitable footwear, as paths may be muddy

WHY DO LEAVES CHANGE COLOUR?

To help you track the onset of autumn colours, the live species and events maps produced by the Woodland Trust's Nature's Calendar project are a great source of information (naturescalendar.woodlandtrust.org.uk). Tree species recorded include beech and oak, with entries for the dates of first autumn tinting, full autumn tinting, first leaves falling and bare tree. By using a slider below the maps, you can see how each event is progressing with time throughout the UK. See page 29 for more on this fascinating project.

Dr Judith Garforth, Citizen Science Officer at the Woodland Trust, sheds more light on why leaves change colour in this blog post:

Autumn is my absolute favourite time of year to be a Nature's Calendar recorder. I love wrapping up warm, getting some fresh air and watching the trees that I monitor for the project gradually changing colour over the season. As we begin to get our 'first autumn tinting' records into Nature's Calendar this year, it's made me stop and wonder why leaves change colour...

Leaves are green in the summer because they contain the green pigment chlorophyll. This pigment is essential for photosynthesis, the process by which plants harness energy from sunlight. As autumn progresses and the trees get ready to shed their leaves, the production of chlorophyll slows down. Any chlorophyll remaining in the leaves is broken

or icy underfoot. Check opening times for historic parks and country estates because some may have reduced hours or already be closed for winter. As with all outdoor activities, be sure to follow the Countryside Code to minimise disturbance to fellow visitors, local residents and wildlife; see page 21 for more details.

Of course, the tree species is another factor in determining when the leaves will change. Trees that lose their leaves in autumn are called deciduous, and include the oak, beech, birch and other native broadleaf species. By contrast, evergreen trees keep their leaves all year; the conifer trees typical of forest plantations are a good example, their narrow, waxy leaves helping to reduce frost and wind damage. However, autumn colours still appear in some, most notably the larch, which puts on a golden yellow display before losing its needles in autumn.

RIGHT Fallen leaves in woods near Thirlmere Reservoir in the Lake District.

down and stored for future use by the tree.

As the amount of green pigment in the leaves reduces, the yellow and orange colours of their carotenoid pigments, which were masked by the chlorophyll during the summer, begin to show. These pigments are thought to help the leaves capture sunlight and protect them from damage by too much light.

Additional autumn leaf colour comes from the red anthocyanin pigment which starts to be produced in leaves during autumn. Like carotenoids, anthocyanin pigments are thought to protect the leaves from damage by excessive light.

If you would like to learn more about our native and imported trees, most bookstores stock tree identification guides and the Woodland Trust website is a fantastic source of information. You might also try smartphone apps, such as the Woodland Trust's Tree ID app and the Seek app from iNaturalist, which is a joint initiative of the California Academy of Sciences and *National Geographic*. Seek uses image recognition to help you analyse your photographs or live images.

WOODS AND FORESTS

Some of Britain's finest autumnal displays occur in woods and forests, particularly where there is a good mix of species. It is the sheer extent and variety that often impresses. Locations with well-known autumnal displays include the Forest of Dean in Gloucestershire, Kielder Water and Forest Park in Northumberland, and Sherwood Forest in Nottinghamshire. Others

ATLANTIC RAINFOREST

Rainforests are normally associated with tropical areas, such as Amazonia, central Africa and parts of Asia. Perhaps surprisingly they also occur in the British Isles, where they are known as Atlantic, Celtic or temperate rainforests. These regions provide rich habitats for birds, mammals and insects, often with impressive displays of lichens, carpets of mosses and rare fungi and plants.

Most are found near western coasts, particularly in Snowdonia, the Lake District and the Scottish Highlands. Here rainfall is high and air temperatures are moderated by the influence of the sea. The mix of tree species varies with location but can include native oak, hazel, ash and birch. They are an increasingly endangered habitat with several projects underway to help secure their future.

ABOVE Dramatic conditions in the northern Lake District, where several pockets of Atlantic rainforest remain.

that are often recommended include Plas Power Woods in Wales, Grizedale Forest and the New Forest in England, Glenariff Forest Park in Northern Ireland, and Glen Affric and the Birks of Aberfeldy in Scotland.

Some of the largest remaining extents of native forest are in the so-called Big Tree Country of Perthshire. This is famed both for the extent of tree coverage and the number of trees notable for their impressive height, girth or age. Queen's View is one destination, as shown at the start of this chapter.

BELOW The Dark Hedges in County Antrim were planted by the Stuart family in the 18th century and consist of a line of beech trees either side of a narrow avenue that once led to a country estate. Their mysterious tangled branches have been much photographed and they featured in the first season of the *Game of Thrones* television series.

HISTORIC PARKS AND COUNTRY ESTATES

For a different type of experience, you might like to visit the more managed grounds of historic parks and country estates. Often surrounding castles or stately homes, larger parks may have miles of woodland walks, still giving the feel of being in the countryside without straying too far from a car park and café. Well-graded wheelchair accessible routes are available at some locations, and lake and riverside walks often provide particularly fine photographic opportunities.

The National Trust manages many such properties. Sites that often make 'best of' lists for autumn colours include Stourhead in Wiltshire and Fountains Abbey in North Yorkshire. Privately owned grounds or stately

homes often figure too, including Rivington Terraced Gardens in Lancashire and Blenheim Palace in Oxfordshire. At some locations, you may be able to combine autumn colour spotting with a trip to see the annual deer rut, for example at Richmond Park in London and at the National Trust sites of Tatton Park in Cheshire and Studley Royal Park in North Yorkshire.

Botanic gardens provide another way to see autumnal colours, including the less familiar shades of imported species. Perhaps the best known are Kew Gardens in London, the Royal Botanic Garden in Edinburgh and the National Botanic Garden of Wales. Most were established for scientific and educational purposes, some more than a century ago. Today, typical roles include education, research and conservation, plus of course providing a great place to visit for tourists and local residents.

Arboretums often have similar objectives but focus on trees, and sometimes shrubs too. Some may be

ABOVE Famous landmarks can be another good place to see autumn colours. Here, they are just starting to appear in the woods around Clifton Suspension Bridge near Bristol. The nearby Clifton Observatory has a café, museum and an amazing view of the Avon Gorge from Giant's Cave, which is reached by a tunnel through the rock.

THE COLOURS OF THE WORLD

Another attraction of botanic gardens and arboretums is the chance to get a flavour of autumn colours from around the world.

Winkworth Arboretum in Surrey is one famous destination. It was created by the horticulturist Dr Wilfrid Fox (1875–1962), who set out to establish a landscape rich with colour, and is now part of the National Trust. Species include Japanese maples, Canadian sugar maples, American Sweet Gum (liquidambar) and Katsura trees, native to Japan and China.

In Scotland, Kilmun Arboretum provides a different type of experience. Managed by Forestry and Land Scotland, over 260 species of tree were planted more than 90 years ago to see how well they would grow in Scottish conditions. Many thrived and over 150 species remain, including Californian sequoia and redwoods, Australian eucalyptus, Japanese cedar and Oregon maple.

Further afield, maple trees produce the fiery red autumnal colours of Japan and New England, which have featured in many a tourist brochure.

part of a larger site, such as at Kew Gardens, while others are independently managed. Places often recommended for anyone on the hunt for autumn colours include Thorp Perrow Arboretum in North Yorkshire, Bedgebury National Pinetum and Forest in Kent, Castlewellan Arboretum in County Down, Westonbirt National Arboretum in Gloucestershire and Bodenham Arboretum in Worcestershire.

ABOVE The exotic autumnal colours of Japanese maple at Castlewellan Arboretum in Northern Ireland.

The sugar maple is the most common variety in the Americas, while the Japanese maple is of course native to Japan. Both are related to the UK's native field maple, which has its own, more muted but beautiful golden yellow display in autumn. Maple displays are also spectacular in Canada – indeed, the maple leaf appears on the national flag. Other species that add to the spectacle in New England include oaks and basswoods, which are known in Europe as lime, while other star Japanese species include ginkgo, rowan, elm, beech, birch and oak.

In the USA, autumn colours are referred to as fall colours or fall foliage, while in Japan they are *koyo*. In Japan, the act of looking for autumn colours is *momijigari*, which means red leaf or maple leaf hunting. The slightly stranger phrase 'leaf peeping' is sometimes used in the USA.

CHAMPION TREES

Another interesting way to see autumn colours is to visit woods that contain champion trees. The Royal Forestry Society defines these as 'individual trees that are important examples of their species because of their enormous size, great age, rarity or historical significance'. Other names include monumental trees or ancient trees.

Incredibly, some trees in the UK have lived for more than 1,000 years, meaning that they were around for the signing of the Magna Carta. Two of the oldest are the Llangernyw Yew in Conwy in Wales and the Ankerwycke Yew at the Runnymede and Ankerwycke Estate, a National Trust property.

There are many other examples, with oaks, yews and sweet chestnuts often topping lists of the oldest trees in the UK. One famous example is the Major Oak in Sherwood Forest, which could be up to 1,000 years old and is reputed to have sheltered Robin Hood in its hollowed-out trunk. In 2014, the public voted it 'Tree of the Year' in a competition run by the Woodland Trust. The annual shortlists from this competition are another good place to look for ideas for special trees to visit, including many ancient and historical examples.

RIGHT The Birnam Oak in Perth and Kinross is said to be one of the last trees remaining from Birnam Wood, which was made famous by William Shakespeare in the play *Macbeth*: 'Macbeth shall never vanquish'd be until Great Birnam Wood to high Dunsinane hill shall come against him'. Like with some other ancient trees, several branches are now supported to prevent them from falling.

CHAPTER 11

WILDFLOWER DISPLAYS

Witness the first snowdrops of the year appear, then walk past carpets of bluebells once spring has arrived. Enjoy spectacular displays of cherry blossom and wildflowers.

Highlights

◆
Anticipate the approach of spring as the first snowdrops appear

◆
Enjoy carpets of bluebells nodding gently in the breeze

◆
See spectacular cherry blossom without travelling to Japan

What you might see

After the dark winter months, wildflowers give some of the first signs that spring is on its way. With wildflowers often being found in beautiful surroundings, spotting them can be part of a great day out.

Snowdrops are usually the first to appear, typically from mid-January to March, depending on weather and location, and sometimes even when there is snow on the ground.

As spring gets underway, bluebells put on a spectacular display, and a sea of blue beneath ancient woodland canopies is a particularly impressive sight. Cherry blossoms appear too, their delicate pink-white flowers providing echoes of the annual *hanami* or flower-viewing festival in Japan.

Level of difficulty ★★

LOCATION can be seen widely throughout the UK
FREQUENCY the best displays may only last a week or two
PREDICTABILITY the time of first flowering varies by type, year and location
SAFETY the normal risks of any outdoor activity

Level ★ for snowdrops and cherry blossom, Level ★★★ for carpets of bluebells

OPPOSITE A carpet of bluebells in woodland in the Lake District.

SNOWDROPS

With their delicate white flowers, snowdrops provide one of the earliest signs of spring. In some winters, they appear while snow is still on the ground. Although widespread, they are not native to the UK and were brought here from central and southern Europe, probably in the 16th century. Their natural habitat includes shady, well-drained soil, particularly in broadleaf woodlands.

Many varieties now exist, some created for gardeners and others cross-pollinating naturally in the wild. The scientific name for the common snowdrop, *Galanthus nivalis*, is derived from the Greek words *gala* (milk) and *anthus* (flower) and the Latin *nivalis* (of the snow), translating roughly as 'milk flower of the snow'. Snowdrop enthusiasts are known as galanthophiles, after the Latin name.

To the expert there are many subtle differences in the size, shape and number of white petal-like shells that surround the heart of each flower. The rarest varieties command surprisingly high prices, and some more exotic types even start flowering in December.

BELOW Common snowdrops in a Scottish woodland setting.

Common snowdrops are found throughout the UK and you often don't have to travel far to see them. However, the time of flowering varies from year to year depending on location and the weather in preceding months, and some displays are only at their best for a week or two. You may therefore need to make more than one visit before success.

Popular viewing destinations include woods, country estates and formal gardens. Some venues impress with the sheer number of flowers, while others dazzle with the many varieties on display. In some places, nature has been helped on its way by the planting of thousands of bulbs, for example in Hyde Park in London and Wallington in Northumberland.

In Scotland, the annual Scottish Snowdrop Festival, organised by Discover Scottish Gardens, includes a wide range of events. In England and Wales, the National Garden Scheme's Snowdrop Festival features more than 100 locations. National Trust and Woodland Trust sites are other popular places to visit.

One thing to watch out for is that some properties only open on specific days because snowdrops flower outside the main tourist season. Also, keep to paths, as snowdrops are easily damaged, and keep dogs and children well away, as the bulb, leaves and stem are toxic.

BLUEBELLS

If snowdrops signal the approach of spring, carpets of bluebells show that it has truly arrived. The most magical experience is to see them in their natural habitat, stretching as far as the eye can see beneath ancient woodland canopies, their sweet scent drifting in a cool breeze. As wildflower expert Sarah Raven states in her book *Wild Flowers:* 'If we did not have bluebell woods, we would travel across the world to see them.'

First flowering is typically during late March and April, starting in the southwest of the UK and progressing to the north. Dates vary by several weeks, depending on whether there has been a warm or cold winter. In woodland, the flowers are typically at their best for about two to three weeks in the short time between the soil starting to warm in spring sunshine and the forest canopy closing overhead.

It is often said that more than half the world's bluebells grow in the UK and most are of the native type, which have delicate indigo-blue flowers with a trumpet shape, their scent and nectar attractive to butterflies and other pollinators. Each plant has a single stem up to 45cm (18in) tall, typically with up to 20 drooping flowers along one side.

While woodland is their most natural setting, one of the UK's most famous bluebell sites is to be found on the open moorland of Rannerdale, a

picturesque valley leading down to the shores of Crummock Water in the Lake District. There was once an ancient woodland here and the bluebells are relics from that time. The site is managed by the National Trust and is a popular tourist destination.

From seed, bluebells take several years for the first flowers to appear and are easily damaged by trampling, so it is important to keep to paths and trails. Most parts of the plant are poisonous, so again keep children and dogs well away. Bluebells are protected under the Wildlife and Countryside Act (1981), and it is illegal to pick, uproot or destroy plants, while landowners are prohibited from removing them from their land to sell.

Spanish bluebells

The native English or British bluebell (the wild hyacinth, or *Hyacinthoides non-scripta*) is widespread in northwestern Europe. However,

FIRST FLOWERING DATES

To track the appearance of wildflowers, the live species and events maps on the Woodland Trust's website are a fabulous tool. They are produced as part of a project called Nature's Calendar (see page 29) to better understand how the seasons unfold for a range of plants and wildlife. Snowdrops and bluebells are included and – for the period 2001 to 2020 – the average first flowering dates were 26 January for snowdrops and 14 April for bluebells. The maps also allow you to see how these dates vary with location, usually showing a clear northward progression with time. The Woodland Trust's blog posts and social media sites are another great source of information, as are those of the National Trust and Wildlife Trusts. More generally, useful social media hashtags for learning about recent sightings include #snowdrops and #bluebells.

it faces a threat from the Spanish Bluebell (*Hyacinthoides hispanica*), which is native to Portugal and western Spain. Introduced as a garden plant, the Spanish Bluebell has spread into the wild, increasingly cross-pollinating with the native species. This results in hybrid species that combine characteristics of both types, thus diluting the gene pool of the native type.

The Spanish Bluebell is easily recognised by its paler, more open flowers, which rather than drooping to one side grow all the way around a more upright stem. It is unscented in contrast to the delightful smell of the native species. Due to this cross-pollination, the UK is now sometimes said to have three species of bluebell: the native type, the Spanish Bluebell and the hybrid variety, in all its many forms.

SPOTTING SNOWDROPS AND BLUEBELLS

When planning a trip to see snowdrops or bluebells it is worth considering the type of day out you fancy. For example, would you like to see flowers in their natural setting, in which case an ancient woodland might be best, or visit a country estate, perhaps with a castle or stately home to visit afterwards and a tearoom or café? Some ideas for places to visit are detailed overleaf.

Country estates

Historic landscaped parks are a feature of the British countryside, often with extensive areas of woodland where wildflowers grow. Some have specific snowdrop or bluebell walks, or even guided trips on certain days, and larger estates may have visitor centres with advice on where to look. Examples include the self-guided bluebell walk at the National Trust's Cliveden property in Buckinghamshire and bluebell days at Hartland Abbey & Gardens in Devon. Some estates have wheelchair and pushchair accessible pathways. Entrance fees are usually charged to help support upkeep, although membership schemes may allow free entry, such as at most National Trust properties and some private estates.

Local woodland

Many towns and cities have woods within easy reach, although you may need to do some online detective work to find out whether snowdrops and bluebells grow there. Paths may range from wide accessible walkways to steep, muddy terrain. Route finding is sometimes more of a challenge with only the occasional sign to help guide the way, although you may be able to download maps or find an information board at a car park. More popular areas may have a visitor or ranger centre. Entrance is often free, but parking is sometimes difficult during the wildflower season so it is important not to spoil things for local residents by blocking roads and gateways, perhaps returning at a quieter time.

Formal gardens

The UK is dotted with many beautiful ornamental gardens open to the public. Here it is often the range of flower species that impresses, although some also have woodlands with snowdrop and bluebell displays. Botanic gardens are another great place to visit, the best known of which are Kew Gardens in London, the Royal Botanic Garden in Edinburgh and the National Botanic Garden of Wales. As with country estates, some have recognised snowdrop or bluebell trails and even guided walks on certain days, plus cafés to retire to afterwards.

Deciding where to go

The map on page 161 includes a wide range of ideas for places to go to see wildflower displays. Many locations have been included as they often score highly in 'best of' lists in national newspaper articles, travel and wildlife magazines and blogs. Before travelling it is always worth checking destination websites for the latest information.

A GLIMPSE INTO WILDFLOWER SCIENCE

Brightly coloured flowers are not just pleasing to the eye but a magnet for bees and butterflies which are attracted by the scents and energy-rich nectar. As pollinators flit among plants, sticky pollen grains attach to their bodies and brush off when they visit other flowers. Pollen grains are often barely visible to the eye; they are roughly the average width of a human hair in bluebells and about half that for snowdrops.

In most plants, the pollen is produced by anthers, which are found on top of stalks within the flower, and together are known as stamen. A more bulbous area at the base is made up of several parts, including the stigma and ovary, whose combined role is to trap and germinate pollen and carry ovules that, once pollinated, develop into seeds.

The fully grown seeds then either drop to the ground or are spread by birds, mammals or the wind. In plants with bulbs – including snowdrops and bluebells – the sugars produced through photosynthesis are stored underground to carry them through to spring, when they flower again. As is often the way in the natural world, there are many exceptions, including plants that self-pollinate and those with male and female parts in separate flowers. Fruit trees such as wild cherries usually propagate when their fruits are eaten by birds or mammals, which then spread the seeds in their travels.

Perhaps surprisingly, ants also play a role in pollinating snowdrop seeds, while bees sometimes steal nectar from bluebells by biting into the base of the flower if they cannot reach inside. Snowdrops also spread via small bulb-like bulbils that grow out from each plant.

However, these suggestions are just a starting point and many people will have other ideas – indeed, some may get quite passionate about why their choice is not included. For example, Kew Gardens is famed for its bluebell displays. You may therefore prefer to do your own research, and the websites of the National Trust, Woodland Trust, Wildlife Trusts, RSPB and various snowdrop festivals are a good starting point. It can also help to read the comments on travel websites, such as Tripadvisor, for feedback from visitors and reports of recent sightings. Finally, wildflowers are fragile, so be sure to follow the Countryside Code (see page 21) when you head out on your trip.

CHERRY BLOSSOM

The delicate blossom of the cherry tree is another sign of spring, most famously in Japan, where the annual *hanami* or flower-viewing festival is held each year. This tradition dates back more than 1,000 years and is a chance for families and friends to meet, walk and picnic against a backdrop of beautiful flowering *sakura* trees. The blossoms symbolise good health, beauty and the ephemeral nature of life.

One of the most popular varieties is the *Somei-Yoshino*, but there are many others too. When planted together these extend the blossoming season, which typically begins in late March in the south of Japan and sometimes

OPPOSITE Some of the much-photographed cherry trees at The Meadows, a large park near the centre of Edinburgh.

ABOVE Damson tree blossom in the Lyth Valley in Cumbria, where damson jam from local orchards is a popular product. Damsons may have been imported from Damascus during the Crusades.

extends into early May in the north. Often the blossoms only remain for a few days, and the national weather forecasting organisation, the Japan Weather Association, publishes forecasts for the dates of first bloom around the nation.

In the UK, the native wild cherry has white blossom, but there are many examples of the Japanese variety in parks and gardens. The Sakura Cherry Tree Project, a joint UK–Japan friendship project, is planting many more in public spaces around the British Isles.

The National Trust also celebrates cherry blossoms through its annual Blossom Watch initiative, which includes other flowering trees too. Check the Trust's website and the hashtag #BlossomWatch on social media for the latest updates. Other types of tree and shrub blossom include the whites of the wild plum, damson, pear tree, hawthorn and blackthorn, and the pinks and whites of the crab apple.

OTHER WILDFLOWERS

Of course, although snowdrops and bluebells are the best known, many other types of wildflowers grow in the British countryside. Estimates vary, but the number of native species is probably several hundred or more if tree

blossoms and flowering shrubs are included. Places to spot wildflowers include woodlands, roadside verges, hedgerows, and coastal, riverside and canal side paths. Typically, the mix of species varies with the local soil type, climate and terrain, but includes familiar field and woodland types, such as the meadow buttercup, wild daffodil, foxglove, common poppy, oxeye daisy and red clover. In coastal and mountain areas, the bright yellow of gorse is a spectacular sight in spring and the delicate purples of bell heather impress in autumn. Many salt-tolerant species thrive in saltmarshes, sand dunes and cliff areas, for example pink thrift and purple sea aster.

Some wildflower species have evocative names, such as the bladder campion or stinking iris, known for its 'meat' smell when the leaves are damaged. The smell of wild garlic, or ramsons, is often a welcome addition when walking through woodland in spring. It can be an indicator of ancient woodland, as are other slow-growing species, such as the wood anemone, red campion and the native bluebell itself.

Others have achieved a certain notoriety, particularly deadly nightshade and Japanese knotweed, a fast-growing, strong-clumping invasive species that can even damage concrete and tarmac (the term invasive or non-native is used to describe troublesome imported species, which sometimes go under the more dramatic name of alien invaders).

Wild orchids provide another type of experience, where the beauty is in the individual flowers rather than their numbers. More than 50 species grow in the UK, although some are so rare that they are carefully protected, their locations known only to a handful of experts.

However, the traditional wildflower meadows of the past are increasingly under threat, many of them lost to intensive farming and urban spread. Encouragingly, though, many land managers now recognise their value not just for aesthetic reasons but as a way to sustain bees, butterflies and other pollinators that support vital parts of the food chain.

Several British sites are world class and in *Wildflower Wonders: The 50 Best Wildflower Sites in the World*, botanist Bob Gibbons mentions two locations in particular. These are the Lizard Peninsula in Cornwall, whose clifftops and valleys blossom in spring, and the low-lying grassy plains (or *machair*) of the Outer Hebrides. Both impress for the huge variety of flowers that appear, with many rare types not found elsewhere. Internationally, other habitats for wildflowers include deserts, prairie grasslands, alpine meadows and high mountain areas.

If you struggle to recognise wildflowers, identification guides are available from most bookstores. Smartphone apps are a handy tool, giving rapid feedback on images and plenty of background information.

CHAPTER **12**

RUTTING DEER

*Watch the mating rituals of red, fallow, sika and roe deer
during the annual deer rut. With luck, maybe see a clash
of antlers as males try to scare off rivals.*

Highlights

◆
Hear the primeval
bellow of a stag at
dawn or dusk

◆
Take a safari to spot
wild deer

◆
Watch mighty stags
clash antlers to fight
off a rival

What you might see

Autumn marks the start of the mating season for Britain's largest land mammal, the red deer, and with it the spectacular sight of their courtship rituals, during which stags lock antlers with rivals and their bellows echo across woods and moors.

The timing of the deer rut varies according to the species, with fallow, sika and red deer rutting in autumn, and roe deer in summer. Country parks give perhaps the best chances of a sighting, but deer can also be spotted in wilder settings across hills, moorland and mountains.

LOCATION ranges from country parks to remote mountain areas
FREQUENCY typically in autumn and early winter
PREDICTABILITY all the usual challenges of predicting wildlife behaviour
SAFETY usual outdoor risks, particularly from deer with young and during the rutting season

Level ★★★ for non-contact behaviour, Level ★★★★★ for clashing antlers (red deer)

BELOW Red deer fighting in Glen Cassley, Scottish Highlands.
© Getty/Heather Leslie Ross

THE RED DEER RUT

In the natural world, the survival of a species often depends on the strongest animals passing on their genes. For deer, this occurs during the annual rut, when stags compete for the chance to mate with hinds.

For the red deer, the fight starts with a bellowing or roaring noise, the length and volume indicating size and strength of the bearer. Sometimes called bolving, it is intended to warn off rivals and attract the interest of potential mates. However, if another male approaches, they may size one another up by strutting alongside each other in a stiff-legged walk known as parallel walking. Other tactics include rolling in urine-soaked mud and collecting vegetation in their antlers by thrashing them along the ground to make themselves appear more intimidating.

If these ritualised behaviours fail, then the fight takes a physical turn, and there is a clash of antlers. Sumo wrestling style, the stags shove each other in an attempt to gain the higher ground and make their opponent stumble or flee. The winner will then chase the rival away, perhaps with a gratuitous stab of the antlers as they depart. Adult stags typically stand over 1m (3.3ft) at the shoulder and weigh up to 200kg. Antlers can span more than a metre across, making them formidable beasts, easily able to scare off weaker rivals. Injuries are therefore common, although rarely fatal.

Red deer tend to mate between late September and early November. As the rutting season approaches, the stag's coat becomes thicker, and physiological changes to the neck and tongue enable them to make a louder bellow or roar. They now become solitary, after living peaceably together outside the rutting season.

During the rut, a stag will adopt a desirable patch of land known as a stand. The strongest may have a so-called harem of several hinds under his protection, although some females move on if not impressed. However, this doesn't stop younger rivals trying to mate while the alpha male is fighting, or resting after a battle.

The time available for mating is rather short, since hinds do not come into season until part way into the rut, and then only for some of the time. This leads to another characteristic stag behaviour of sniffing the air to find hinds in season. Seeing their lips and nostrils flare makes for an impressive sight.

After the rut ends, stags and hinds go their separate ways, with the hinds forming larger groups. Winter coats are shed in spring and then calves are born in early summer as temperatures warm, increasing their chances of survival. Antlers are also shed in spring, only to grow again in time for the next rutting season. The new growth is initially covered by a layer of skin

called velvet, which is shed once they are fully grown, often through rubbing against trees and vegetation.

SAFETY TIPS FOR VIEWING DEER

Despite their usually placid nature, deer are large animals that can cause injuries, particularly during the rut and when protecting their young. Their natural behaviour can also be disrupted by spectators approaching too close, causing stress and possibly injury to the animal as they try to flee.

Typical advice includes keeping quiet and out of sight and, if possible, not approaching from an upwind direction. Most importantly of all, keep your distance: the advice is usually to keep at least 50–100m (about 150–300ft) between yourself and the deer. Binoculars or a camera with a zoom lens can help give a better view. Dogs should, of course, be kept well away, ideally at home, but if not, on a short lead. Never attempt to feed deer.

For more viewing tips, the British Deer Society publishes a very useful code of conduct that covers social, environmental and individual responsibilities. Most venues with deer also have advice on their websites or at the site, including any local regulations that must be followed. Even in a park, distances can be large, so you should wear appropriate clothing and footwear for what may be a long walk in autumnal or early winter conditions, taking a drink and snack too. A map helps, as it is easy to get lost when following paths through woods and across grassland.

Deer are often said to be at their most active after dawn and before dusk. For early morning visits in particular, the grass may be soaked with mist still lingering near the ground, while it is advisable to take a torch at dusk. This all adds to the adventure if suitable precautions are taken.

BELOW Adult red deer at Beecraigs Country Park in Scotland.

THE MONARCH OF THE GLEN

The Monarch of the Glen (1851) by Sir Edwin Landseer is one of the most famous artworks of its day. The painting depicts a magnificent red deer stag against a backdrop of mist-covered Highland mountains. During the 19th century it became a Scottish icon with reproductions appearing widely in tourist adverts and brochures. The original now hangs in the Scottish National Gallery in Edinburgh.

Landseer's stag has a magnificent set of antlers with 12 pointed tips, known as tines. This is typical of a mature stag, as they gain more branches and tines over the years. In wild Scottish deer, the maximum is typically 16, although more have been recorded.

In the Victorian era, a stag with 12 points was known as a Royal and the names Imperial and Monarch were reserved for those with 14 and 16 points. Not all stags with this many points made the grade, as there were additional criteria regarding the symmetry of antlers.

COUNTRY ESTATES AND NATURE RESERVES

Deer are found in a huge range of habitat types, from small enclosures to wild mountain regions. However, visiting a country estate is one of the best ways to see them in a fairly natural setting. Many estates were first stocked in medieval times for venison and game hunting, and although their overall range is limited by walls or fences, estate deer may still have surprisingly large areas of woodland and grassland in which to roam.

For novice deer spotters, advice may be on hand at visitor centres, and some have recommended deer walks, such as those at Studley Royal Park in North Yorkshire, a National Trust property. These trails can be surprisingly long, several miles in some cases, but after the exertion there is usually a stately home or castle to visit nearby, with a café in the grounds.

In London, Richmond Park provides a good example. Created at the command of Charles I in the 17th century, it is the city's largest Royal Park and home to more than 600 red and fallow deer. Although several roads pass through the park, you can still walk miles along woodland and grassland tracks. The park is a national nature reserve and other highlights include the woods and wildflowers of Isabella Plantation, the lakes of Pen Ponds and magnificent views of the Thames Valley. There is a café near the visitor information centre.

Further north, Tatton Park in Cheshire is another well-known destination for spotting deer. Other highlights include a mansion, gardens and farm. Organised deer walks or rides are sometimes advertised. Other historic sites with deer herds include Margam Castle in south Wales, Holkham Hall in Norfolk and Powderham Castle in Devon, and the National Trust sites of Dinefwr in south Wales and Knole Park in Kent; check online that sites are open before travelling.

In Scotland, places to see deer include the Highland Wildlife Park, run by the Royal Zoological Society of Scotland, and Beecraigs Country Park, managed by West Lothian Council. In Northern Ireland, Gosford Forest Park is managed by Armagh City, Banbridge and Craigavon Borough Council.

Whichever type of park or reserve you visit, one thing to bear in mind is that the deer rut occurs towards the end of the main tourist season, so there may be restrictions on opening times. It is therefore worth checking

RSPB NATURE RESERVES

Several RSPB reserves are also home to deer herds, including Minsmere in Suffolk, which has one of the largest populations. As Ian Barthorpe, visitor experience officer at RSPB Minsmere, said:

The annual red deer rut is one of the greatest wildlife spectacles in the UK, and watching it a truly sensory experience. The rut is a show of strength by the dominant testosterone-fuelled stags as they battle for supremacy and the right to mate with as many hinds as possible, which they gather into groups known as harems.

Antler to antler battles are rare, as the stags try to avoid physical combat for risk of injury from those impressive antlers. Instead, they display their strength and power through a series of almost ritualised moves, including parallel walking and brief chases, and proclaim their dominance with deep, almost prehistoric bellows. Scent plays a big part too, with the stags urinating to mark their territories and tasting the air to determine whether the hinds are ready to mate.

The action peaks around dawn and dusk during October, and can be watched from public footpaths on Westleton Heath. An even better option is to book onto the RSPB's popular 4x4 deer safaris, joining a knowledgeable guide to get closer to the action and experience the true power of the rut.

ABOVE Three red deer stags in the mountains of the Cairngorms National Park.
© Getty/Javier Fernández Sánchez

relevant websites where the deer rut is specifically mentioned for the latest information, particularly if a dawn or late afternoon visit is envisaged.

WILDERNESS AREAS

Beyond the confines of a park or reserve, it becomes more challenging to spot deer, but a wild sighting offers an extra sense of achievement. The Scottish Highlands are perhaps the most famous destination for wild deer; others include parts of Exmoor, the Peak District and the Lake District.

In the wild, a deer's natural range extends many miles and they are more wary of people. In prehistoric times, predation from wolves would have been a factor and, while these are long gone in the UK, this remains a risk in some parts of the USA and continental Europe. However, one challenge that Scottish deer still have to face is midges.

In mountain areas, deer typically move to higher ground in summer, then return to valleys in winter for food and shelter. In recent decades, the Isle of Rum Red Deer Project has helped greatly with understanding their behaviour. Led by a consortium of universities headed by the University of Edinburgh, the project began in the 1950s and has tracked deer populations over many generations in a wild environment. The project's website is a fascinating source of information on deer behaviour.

Other Scottish locations with large concentrations of deer include the

Isle of Jura, the Isle of Arran and the Cairngorms National Park. As described later, guided trips provide the best chances of a sighting in this type of terrain.

OTHER TYPES OF DEER

Although much of this chapter is about Britain's largest species – red deer – there is another native species. This is the smaller roe deer, which has a red-brown coat in summer that turns grey or pale brown in winter. Like red deer, their favoured habitat is woodland, but they are also common in open grassland and moorland.

Four other species are found in the wild but were introduced from abroad. Fallow deer are the longest established and were probably brought from the Mediterranean region in the 11th century. Sika, muntjac and Chinese water deer are more recent arrivals, having been imported from Asia in the 19th and 20th centuries.

Fallow deer often have distinctive white-spotted tan coats, while sika deer coats range from pale cream to dark brown. However, exceptions occur, with some fallow deer almost completely white or black. Both are of a similar size, between that of roe and red deer.

ABOVE Antelope in the savannah in east Africa.

Muntjac and Chinese water deer are smaller, and the former grows sharp canine teeth or incisors, earning them the slightly alarming nickname of 'vampire deer', which is out of kilter with their relatively unthreatening behaviour.

Distribution maps provided by the British Deer Society show red deer hotspots in much of Scotland, Cumbria, East Anglia, southwest England and parts of Northern Ireland. Roe deer are even more widespread, except in parts of Kent, central England, Wales and Northern Ireland.

The remaining species are less widely distributed, with sika found in isolated pockets throughout the British Isles, and fallow most common as far north as Yorkshire and Lancashire. Muntjac tend to be spotted mainly in central and southern England, while Chinese water deer have an even more limited range, typically being found mainly in East Anglia and the home counties.

As with size and appearance, rutting behaviour varies widely between species. For example, male fallow deer often compete in groups to attract female deer (does). In contrast, the roe deer rut occurs mainly in July and August and is more likely to result in injuries. Sika deer make perhaps the largest range of sounds during the rut, including grunts, barks and whistles.

GOING ON SAFARI

Particularly in wilderness areas, if you're new to deer watching perhaps the best chance of seeing the rut is on a guided trip with an expert. Trips are either on foot or via off-road vehicle, such as those sometimes offered on Exmoor and in the Scottish Highlands. Guided trips are also available at RSPB Minsmere (see page 194) and at some National Trust properties and private estates: check websites for the latest details.

In Swahili, safari simply means journey or trip, but in recent decades it has also come to mean an organised wildlife spotting tour. In Africa, this is usually to see the so-called 'Big Five' of lion, leopard, elephant, rhinoceros and buffalo. Antelopes are also popular and species include impala, kudu and wildebeest.

Deer are part of the same scientific order (artiodactyla) as antelopes, although they belong to a different family (cervidae). A key difference is that both male and female antelopes (bovidae) in most species grow horns continuously, whereas deer have evolved to grow new antlers each year, possibly in case they are damaged in the annual rut.

MEDIEVAL DEER PARKS

During medieval times, deer populations increased for a most unusual reason. This was the creation of royal hunting forests, to provide venison for the king's table and hold hunting parties to reward loyal subjects. Many were established in the 11th century by William the Conqueror after the Norman conquest. Under a new and widely hated Forest Law, land could be seized to create protected areas where deer and wild boar could roam. The word 'forest' differed from the modern usage as it could cover any area of suitable habitat, including heathland, moorland and woodland.

Fallow deer were introduced to the UK around this time, and red and roe deer populations surged. More than 25 royal forests were established, protecting huge swathes of land, including the Forest of Dean, the New Forest, and Sheringham Forest of Robin Hood fame.

Hunting rights were closely guarded, with severe, often brutal, punishments for poaching. The grazing and farming rights of local inhabitants were greatly restricted, but some were restored by the Magna Carta of 1215 and the Charter of the Forest, two years later. This included some moderation of the punishments allowed.

The royal hunting forests started to decrease in popularity in the 14th century, but deer parks remained a status symbol and were often attached to stately homes and manor houses. Landowners would receive a 'licence to empark' from the Crown. Some occurred in what today seem the most

ABOVE Fallow deer at Richmond Park in London.

RIGHT Deer viewed from a distance disappearing into the woods in Richmond Park, London.

unlikely locations, including the Royal Park at Toxteth in Liverpool, which once extended north to the city centre through what are now built-up areas. The Royal Parks of London were also founded during this period.

It was only in the 17th century that deer parks began to decline, with some falling into disrepair and others having their status removed for grazing, residential and industrial use. Many of those that remain are now managed by the National Trust, private estates and the Royal Parks in London.

Salmon runs
Wild waterfalls
Sunken villages chapter

Smoo Cave

Falls of Shin
Loch Glascarnoch

Falls of Glomach

Linn of Tummel
Steall Falls
Pitlochry Dam
Buchanty Spout

Grey Mare's Tail
Philiphaugh Estate
Kielder Water
Bushmills
Hexham Weir

Aira Force
High Force
Haweswater Reservoir
Hardraw Force
Cautley Spout
Gaping Gill
Spelga Reservoir
Ingleton Falls
Thruscross Reservoir
Stainforth Force

Formby Beach
Ladybower Reservoir

Aber Falls
Llyn Celyn
Rutland Water
Lake Vyrnwy

Borth & Ynyslas
Craig Goch Reservoir
Elan Valley
Cenarth Falls
Dan yr Ogof
Clydach Gorge
Henrhyd Falls
Pontsticill Reservoir

Weald & Downland
Living Museum

Burrator Reservoir

Hallsands

WATER

CHAPTER 13

SALMON RUNS

Marvel as salmon leap waterfalls and weirs as they head upstream to their spawning grounds. Take on the challenge of trying to photograph a salmon in mid air.

Highlights

◆
Watch for the flash of a salmon leaping a waterfall

◆
Cheer salmon on their way as they try to climb a weir

◆
Test your photographic skills to the limit

What you might see

After starting life in a mountain stream, salmon head for the ocean, returning one or more years later to spawn. This is the remarkable life cycle of the Atlantic salmon, whose return journey can involve jumping weirs and waterfalls, making for a spectacular sight.

Spotting their leaps can be a challenge, and photographing them even more so, requiring both patience and luck. Viewing salmon at a weir is easier, and you may see the occasional jump as fish head on their way.

Level of difficulty ★★★★

LOCATION seen mainly in northern and western mountain areas
FREQUENCY often best in autumn following heavy rainfall
PREDICTABILITY some indicators, but with many factors at play
SAFETY normal outdoor risks, particularly on slippery paths near fast-flowing water

Level ★★★ for fish pass and river sightings, Level ★★★★★ for leaping salmon

OPPOSITE Migrating salmon are seen leaping at Buchanty Spout on the River Tay in Perthshire on 22 October 2020. The salmon are returning upstream from the sea, where they have spent between two and four winters feeding, with many covering huge distances to return to the fresh waters to spawn. © Getty/Jeff J Mitchell/Staff

PREVIOUS PAGES The Falls of Clyde in the upper reaches of the River Clyde.

AQUATIC HIGH JUMPERS

Imagine waiting beside a waterfall or cascade as water crashes down to the stream below. Suddenly a flash appears as a salmon leaps into the air, before falling back into the torrent. More appear, only to fail again, until suddenly one manages to clear the jump and continue its journey upstream, earning applause from any spectators nearby.

These remarkable leaps are just a tiny part of the extraordinary life cycle of the Atlantic salmon, which began at least a year before in a mountain stream. In between, they have visited the west Atlantic or Norwegian seas to feed on the rich prey in those waters, before returning fully grown to the same river to spawn, leaping over obstacles in their path.

Like a high jumper, they need a run-up first, ideally with a pool of water to gain speed. The largest salmon are thought to reach maximum (burst) speeds of 24–32km/h (15–20mph), although colder temperatures slow them down, and leaps of 2–3m (7–10ft) are common.

Sometimes nature is given a helping hand in the form of fish passes (see page 206). These watery ladders allow the fish to climb past dams and weirs without leaping, although with luck you may still see the occasional splash or jump as instinct kicks in.

BELOW A salmon is seen leaping up the flowing waters of Stainforth Force waterfall near Settle in the Yorkshire Dales on 21 October 2021, to return to its spawning grounds.
© Getty/OLI SCARFF/Contributor

Where and when to go

Salmon rivers are most common in Scotland, northern England, Wales and Northern Ireland, and if you search online, you will find a choice of locations where leaps occur. Some of the most popular waterfalls include:

- **Buchanty Spout** – on the River Almond near Crieff (Perth and Kinross)
- **Cenarth Falls** – on the River Teifi in southwest Wales (Ceredigion)
- **Falls of Shin** – on the River Shin in northern Scotland (Sutherland)
- **Linn of Tummel** – on the River Garry north of Pitlochry (Perth and Kinross)
- **Stainforth Force** – on the River Ribble near Settle (Yorkshire)

Visitor websites and blog posts often describe how to reach the site and what to expect. What is more difficult is to say precisely when to go, which is why this spectacle has been given the highest level of difficulty. However, some general guidelines can be sketched out. Autumn is often the best time, with October and November typical for certain sites. However, on some rivers, particularly in Scotland, the salmon run begins in spring, for example at the Falls of Shin. Timings and numbers vary from year to year, so check relevant websites for the latest information.

For the best leaping conditions, salmon often move upstream after a period of heavy rainfall and hence into deeper water at waterfalls and cascades. They typically set off once a burst of freshwater appears, provided that water temperatures are high enough to tempt them inland. Before jumping, they often wait for flows to drop slightly from the peak to allow time for sediment to settle, giving better visibility underwater. For the more technically minded visitors, current and forecast water levels are available online for some rivers where salmon leap: see the websites of the relevant monitoring agencies (Environment Agency in England, Natural Resources Wales, Scottish Environment Protection Agency and the Rivers Agency in Northern Ireland).

At many destinations, the combination of high flows and spray can make access difficult. Sometimes this involves crossing slippery paths or rocks close to fast-moving water. You therefore need to take great care, and wear appropriate footwear and wet weather gear. Wrap up warm for the wait, and it's a good idea to take a fully charged phone and let someone know your plans in case you run into problems.

ARTIFICIAL OBSTACLES

In some rivers, weirs present an obstacle to salmon but are still low enough to be leapt across. Hexham Weir, for example, lies on the River Tyne near

the centre of Hexham in Northumberland. However, others stop migration completely so, as at Hexham, fish passes are increasingly installed to help salmon and other migratory fish on their journey upstream. These come in many forms but typically consist of a series of steps, although some try to mimic the form of a natural channel. Not surprisingly, many salmon choose this easier route, so the most likely spectacle is of fish beneath the water. However, you may see the occasional splash or leap if conditions are right. As with waterfalls, visitor information websites are the best place to check before venturing out.

A popular example is Pitlochry Dam and Salmon Ladder, which was built near the centre of the town of Pitlochry, in Perth and Kinross, between 1947 and 1951. The ladder was specially constructed to allow more than 5,000 salmon per year to clear the massive obstacle and return to their spawning grounds. It incorporates 34 chambers and three larger pools where fish can rest before moving higher. Screens keep large fish away from the dam's

LEFT Buchanty Spout in Perth and Kinross, a popular spot for trying to see leaping salmon.

BELOW A part-submerged salmon trying to swim upstream at Murray Cauld on the River Ettrick. This fish or another leapt dramatically into the air at around this time, glinting in the winter sunshine.

hydropower turbines, but smaller fish can pass downstream unharmed. Some readers may remember an underwater salmon viewing area here, but this has since been replaced by an outdoor display next to the fish ladder. The visitor centre also has a display on the life cycle of salmon as part of a wider exhibition on energy generation.

Further south, the Salmon Viewing Centre at Philiphaugh Estate includes a video feed of salmon passing nearby Murray Cauld, a weir built in the 19th century on Ettrick Water to divert water for local mills. A small-scale hydro-electric station has been installed here in recent years with a fish pass alongside, but salmon still try leaping the weir. There is an imaginative display on the salmon, local wildlife and environmental issues in the centre, and additional highlights nearby include a walled garden, café and woodland walks.

In some river basins, restocking has given nature another helping hand, particularly on the River Tyne, which is now one of the best salmon rivers in

AN INCREDIBLE JOURNEY

At around 1m (3.3ft) long, a fully grown Atlantic salmon is an impressive beast. Its journey to the sea typically begins in the gravel beds of mountain streams, where the recently hatched fish take shelter. Known as alevins, they feed off an attached yolk sac before emerging as juvenile fish, or fry. Now feeding on aquatic insects and other small invertebrates, they soon develop a patterned camouflage, at which stage they are known as parr. Parr usually remain upstream for a year or more, particularly in cooler northern waters where prey is less plentiful.

Migration typically begins in spring or early summer, with fish gaining a silver sheen to provide better camouflage in ocean waters. Now known as smolts, their prey at sea includes sand eels, shrimp, sprats and herring. Favoured destinations include the western Atlantic, western Greenland and the seas around Norway, where the smolts rapidly gain weight in the rich feeding grounds.

The fully grown adult fish typically return after one to three years, usually to the same river they spawned in. This remarkable feat is thought to be due to their keen sense of smell for minerals and other tracers in the water. Salmon that return after a year or so at sea are known as grilse. They are smaller and arrive later in the year than multi-year salmon. As a species, this staggered return probably helps salmon withstand droughts and other natural disasters that could wipe out an entire river's population.

After gathering in estuaries, the trigger to swim upstream is often a spate of high flows. However, water temperatures, tide levels and water quality are also factors. Once in a river, early arrivals may spend months in deep pools before finishing their journey, waiting for spawning conditions to be just right. The chemicals released by sexually mature fish (pheromones) may be another trigger.

Spawning usually occurs once waters are cooler, starting in early winter, with hatching in early spring. A female (hen) salmon typically lays thousands of eggs in a hollow made with her tail, known as a redd. These are then fertilised immediately by the male (cock) salmon, before being covered again. Sexually mature parr may also contribute.

Salmon favour well oxygenated clean streams, with vegetated and tree-lined banks to provide cover, and woody debris to shelter insects and other prey. It is an incredible thought that, during the spawning season, ocean-going predators may be lurking just beneath the surface of some mountain streams, having travelled thousands of miles and climbed hundreds of feet or more to get there. However, evolution has meant that, as small streams cannot possibly provide enough food, the adults hardly feed once back in freshwater, so only a small proportion survive to spawn again. Remarkably this means that returning salmon are a rich source of protein for upland rivers, helping to sustain other species as well as their young.

Atlantic salmon are found across Europe, from Spain and Portugal to Scandinavia and Greenland. In the British Isles, they spawn in many upland regions, except in much of central and southeastern England. Smaller numbers occur in the northeast USA and Canada, where various species of Pacific salmon are dominant, of which the chinook (king) and sockeye salmon are probably best known.

Threats to salmon include pollution, disease, overfishing, predation and siltation of spawning grounds. In river headwaters, actions that can help to encourage spawning include planting native trees along riverbanks, keeping cattle away to reduce erosion, and removing weirs and other barriers to migration, or building fish passes alongside.

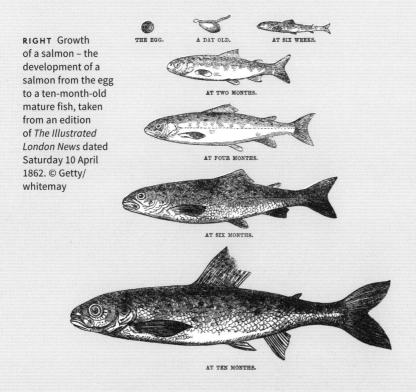

RIGHT Growth of a salmon – the development of a salmon from the egg to a ten-month-old mature fish, taken from an edition of *The Illustrated London News* dated Saturday 10 April 1862. © Getty/whitemay

THE EGG.   A DAY OLD.   AT SIX WEEKS.

AT TWO MONTHS.

AT FOUR MONTHS.

AT SIX MONTHS.

AT TEN MONTHS.

the UK. Kielder Salmon Centre was built to compensate for the building of Kielder Water, one of the UK's largest reservoirs, which cut off part of the spawning grounds in the basin. There is a visitor information centre on site, and Kielder Observatory is nearby (see page 43).

In Northern Ireland, the River Bush Salmon Station in Bushmills is another centre for salmon research, where scientists have investigated population dynamics for many years. The river, one of the best in Northern Ireland for salmon, meets the coast close to the unusual geological formations of the Giant's Causeway.

EELS, LAMPREY AND SEA TROUT

The Atlantic salmon is not the only fish species to migrate to these shores. Anadromous species such as eels, sea lamprey and sea trout spend part of their lives in inland freshwater and the rest at sea.

In contrast to salmon, European eels start their journey in the ocean, in the warm waters of the Sargasso Sea in the western Atlantic. The larvae then drift east, metamorphosing into young eels in the process. At this stage, they

BELOW Pitlochry Dam with several steps in the fish ladder visible to the left of the image.

RIGHT Close-up of a salmon that forms part of the sculpture 'The Waters of the River Bush' in Bushmills. It was designed by Holger Christian Lönze.

BELOW The outlet weir at Windermere in the Lake District. The green-coloured ramp is a bristle strip to help eels head upstream.

13 . SALMON RUNS

are almost transparent and known as glass eels. It is only on moving inland that they gain their more familiar dark colour. Bristle strips are sometimes installed at weirs to help eels on their journey inland, the flexible spikes allowing them to wriggle their way upstream. Now known as elvers, they remain inland for several years before returning to the sea. Here, like salmon, they gain a silver sheen for better camouflage in ocean waters. Their journey ends back at the Sargasso Sea, where they reproduce and die.

Rather more fierce, the adult sea lamprey looks similar to an eel but has teeth and uses its sucker to attach to other fish to suck their blood. Thanks to this parasitic behaviour, they are sometimes called 'vampire fish' or 'vampires of the deep'. After spawning, the larvae grow in the river bed, before metamorphosing into the adult form and heading out to sea. Sea lamprey are one of the most primitive species of fish, as are their river-dwelling cousins the river and brook lamprey.

Similar to salmon, at first sight sea trout can be difficult to tell apart, but adults are generally smaller, and more survive after spawning. Juvenile fish again develop a silvery appearance in the ocean and return after a few months or more, but not necessarily to the same river. Back inland, their colour changes yet again, making them hard to distinguish from the smaller brown trout, a freshwater fish only living inland.

URBAN SALMON

Although wild salmon are under threat in many places, some environmental achievements offer hope, for example on the River Mersey. The river flows down from the Peak District to the coast near Liverpool, passing through heavily industrialised areas on the way. Until the industrial revolution, salmon were part of the staple diet for local communities, with the surplus even used as animal feed. In a 1697 letter to Richard Norris of Speke, published in *The Norris Papers*, local industrialist Thomas Patten wrote:

> *I am informed that there is a design to bring a bill into the House of Commons against fish wears that hinder Navigation, in Navigable Rivers, and that take, and destroy fish, and the fry of fish. You very well know the mischief that is done in the River Mercy, or at least have frequently heard, what vast numbers of Salmon Trout are taken, so as to supply all of the Country, and Market Towns 20 miles around, and when the Country is cloyed, or when they cannot get sale for them, they give them to their swine...*

However, pollution from sewage and chemical works led to the salmon's demise and numbers reached a low point in the 20th century. As water quality and fisheries expert PD Jones wrote in the magazine *SourceNW*:

> *Everyone living on Merseyside was well aware of the dreadful conditions in the river – indeed, local folklore insisted that it was impossible to drown in the Mersey as one would be poisoned first.*

Since that time, the situation has been transformed thanks to the many individuals and organisations who contributed to the 25-year-long Mersey Basin Campaign. One key factor was to recognise the link between water quality and economic regeneration, with Liverpool's waterfront in particular now one of the most spectacular in the world.

Fish populations have also recovered, and salmon have been sighted south of Manchester and in the Peak District in recent years. The Mersey Rivers Trust and other organisations continue to improve the river basin environment.

PHOTOGRAPHING LEAPING SALMON

Some of the most impressive photographs of leaping salmon show them mid-flight against a backdrop of whitewater, with head-on images particularly striking. One of the most widely recommended techniques for capturing salmon mid-flight is to wait a while to see where most are leaping, and then to keep the camera pointed at and focused on that spot. A tripod may help, with a remote release so you don't have to stare at the screen or viewfinder for long periods. If your camera allows, manual focusing may result in a sharper image, and continuous shooting gives more chance of a salmon in shot.

As salmon sail by, the temptation is to try to follow them with the camera, but be patient and continue to focus on your chosen spot. However, some report good results by panning and focusing as fish leap, although this is more challenging to do successfully.

Another tip is to make yourself as comfortable as possible; if you need to look up or walk away for a break, the largest salmon are sure to choose that time to leap! Take warm clothing, snacks and drinks, and find a safe, dry spot to wait. Try to be fair to other photographers too, by not hogging the best spots all day.

CHAPTER 14

SUNKEN VILLAGES

See the remains of flooded villages during a drought and the buildings that were saved when reservoirs were built. Look for signs of prehistoric forests and footprints around the coast.

Highlights

◆
See long lost
villages reappear from
beneath the waves

◆
Visit medieval
buildings rescued
when a reservoir
was built

◆
Walk through
the remains of a
prehistoric forest

What you might see

While not matching the romance of the lost city of Atlantis, sunken villages hold a genuine fascination and belong to the real world rather than that of legend. Their secrets are typically revealed as reservoirs drop to unusually low levels during droughts, exposing ruins not seen for many years. Most were

flooded during the reservoir building boom that began in Victorian times and continued well into the 20th century. Particularly treasured buildings were sometimes relocated.

Other surprising sights around our shores include the remains of coastal forests that reappear following storms, and the preserved footsteps of hunter gatherers exposed at low tide.

BELOW Haweswater Reservoir at a time of low levels, exposing some of the drystone walls of Mardale Green village.

SUNKEN VILLAGES

During the 1800s, the need for clean water increased as towns and cities grew, with reservoirs an obvious way to meet that demand. The prime sites were in the valleys of hilly areas such as the Peak District, Dartmoor, the Lake District and the Yorkshire Dales. In some cases, villages and farms stood in the way and were flooded during construction, with their residents moved to other areas.

These relocations continued well into the 20th century. Many sad stories abound of those who lost their homes and the social and economic upheaval this caused, but some people found a better way of life.

Today, few signs of these villages remain, other than the occasional information panel describing the history of the construction of a reservoir. However, when water levels drop during a drought, roads and walls may reappear, and sometimes even bridges and buildings. These provide both a fascinating sight and the chance to reflect on the sacrifices made many years ago.

Mardale Green

One of the most famous drowned locations is the farming village of Mardale Green in Cumbria. Set at the end of a spectacular valley surrounded by high peaks, the village was flooded during the construction of Haweswater Reservoir. This raised the level of the natural lake in the valley by almost 30m (98ft), nearly tripling its area.

Haweswater Reservoir is now part of an extensive system of reservoirs and pipelines that supplies much of Cumbria, and parts of Lancashire and Greater Manchester via a 109km (68-mile) long pipeline called the Haweswater Aqueduct. The aqueduct was completed in the 1950s and featured in the unexpected hit television series *Sewermen*,

RIGHT Some of the drystone walls and lanes that surrounded Mardale Green, which reappeared when water levels dropped in 2021.

WATER

which described the dangerous task of inspecting its inner workings for the first time since construction. The engineers who did the work received special training in a simulation facility and were dubbed 'aquanauts'.

The reservoir was filled in the early 1940s after the buildings at Mardale Green had been flattened along with those at Measand, a smaller settlement further down the valley. Mardale's Holy Trinity Church was deconsecrated and its graveyard exhumed and relocated to the nearby village of Shap. The

ABOVE Remains of Derwent village exposed due to low levels at Ladybower Reservoir in July 2022. © Getty/Anthony Devlin/Bloomberg/Contributor

SOME TIPS ON VISITING SUNKEN VILLAGES

Keep an eye on local news and social media; developing drought and low water levels often generate stories of a local 'Atlantis' emerging from the depths.

For the more technically minded, most water companies publish situation reports on their websites, often comparing current conditions to past events. Monthly water situation reports published by the Environment Agency include a summary and commentary on current reservoir storage levels in England. These sometimes refer to the volume of water stored as the 'stock' in percentage terms.

If you make a visit, it is both respectful and common sense to remain on solid ground above the high-water mark of the reservoir and not to attempt to visit the ruins. In 2018, a mountain rescue team was called out to extract a man stuck in mud near the ruins at Ladybower Reservoir and another rescue occurred at Capel Celyn in 2022. In addition to deep, soft mud, other potential hazards include hidden or submerged wires, metal and rocks.

church's interior fittings went to two others in the region, and the stone and windows were used to help build the reservoir's water draw-off tower, an elegant structure closer to the dam.

Lanes and drystone walls that once surrounded fields have appeared several times in recent decades. More rarely, as levels drop further, the remains of Chapel Bridge, a traditional stone bridge near the centre of the village, have emerged.

Ladybower Reservoir

Equally dramatic sights occur during droughts at Ladybower Reservoir in the Peak District. This is the lowermost of three reservoirs along the Upper Derwent Valley, built to supply towns and cities in the Midlands and Sheffield in South Yorkshire. During construction in the 1940s, the historic villages of Derwent and Ashopton were flooded, causing considerable controversy at the time. Buildings at Derwent included a school, church and the 17th-century Derwent Hall. Parts of the village have reappeared several times in recent decades.

Other flooded secrets

Other reservoirs around the British Isles that occasionally reveal their secrets include:

- **Burrator Reservoir** on Dartmoor, where the remains of a village wall reappear, and it is thought that a bridge and farmhouse might one day appear during extreme low levels
- **Llyn Celyn and Lake Vyrnwy** in Wales, where the remains of buildings sometimes reappear – these are associated with the village of Capel Celyn and the original site of Llanwddyn village before it was relocated
- **Loch Glascarnoch** between Ullapool and Inverness, where the remains of an old road with two bridges are occasionally revealed
- **Spelga Reservoir** in the Mourne Mountains in Northern Ireland, where an old mountain road sometimes emerges
- **Thruscross Reservoir** in Yorkshire, where the remains of a flax mill and other buildings from 17th-century West End village reappear

Several of these reservoirs reached unusually low levels during the prolonged dry weather in the summer of 2022.

RELOCATED BUILDINGS

In the case of some reservoirs, a different approach was taken during construction, which involved rescuing historically significant buildings or structures before they were flooded.

Perhaps the most remarkable effort was at Bough Beech Reservoir in Kent, where two medieval farm buildings were saved. These were the 16th-century Winkhurst Tudor Kitchen, once a wing of a larger manor house, and the 15th-century Bayleaf Farmhouse, an impressive timber-framed hall-house.

In the late 1960s, both buildings were moved brick by brick and timber by timber to the newly established Weald & Downland Living Museum near Chichester in Sussex. This fascinating place is home to more than 50 historic buildings from across southern England, ranging from medieval times to the Victorian era. The Tudor Kitchen was the first building at the museum and, along with the Bayleaf Farmhouse, remains one of its most popular sights. The museum holds regular demonstrations and courses in traditional trades and crafts, bringing Sussex's rural past to life.

At the reservoir itself, the picturesque Oast House near the dam once

OPPOSITE Normanton Church at Rutland Water.

ABOVE The Bayleaf Farmhouse at the Weald & Downland Living Museum.

housed a visitor centre; information boards in a nearby historic barn still describe the history of the area. With nature reserves and scenic views, the reservoir is popular with anglers, walkers and birdwatchers.

At Rutland Water near Leicester, the much-photographed Normanton Church was saved using a different approach. Originally built on the site of a medieval church, its tower was replaced in the 19th century with the distinctive structure in the Corinthian style still seen today. When the reservoir was built in the 1970s, the floor of the church was raised, following a local outcry, and an embankment constructed around it to form an island, which is connected to the shore by a short causeway. Now owned by Anglian Water, the church is a popular wedding venue. The reservoir – the largest in England by surface area – is a scenic spot popular with mountain bikers, anglers, birdwatchers and watersports enthusiasts.

Several other less dramatic examples can be found around the British Isles, including the items from Mardale Holy Trinity Church noted on pages 216–19 and a historic packhorse bridge, moved brick by brick when Ladybower Reservoir was built.

SUNKEN COASTAL VILLAGES

Although this chapter focuses on villages lost beneath reservoirs, sunken villages can also be found around the coast. Here, storms are the main culprit, sometimes causing buildings or even entire settlements to be lost to the sea.

Perhaps the most famous is Dunwich, which in medieval times was one of the largest port towns in England. However, due to repeated storms in the 13th and 14th centuries, the harbour became unusable and many buildings were swept away. Using the latest marine survey technology, research led by the University of Southampton has shown many signs of the original town beneath the waves, including ruined churches and port buildings.

In south Devon, the small fishing village of Hallsands was lost for another reason. Situated on a natural rock platform above a shingle beach, by the end of the 19th century it had 37 houses and a pub. However, from 1897 a dredging company had been excavating shingle from an area just to the north for use in dock building in Plymouth. This affected currents and erosion along the coast, but warnings from local residents were initially ignored. Eventually the dredging company was ordered to improve sea defences in the village and their licence was finally revoked in 1902. However, houses continued to be damaged and despite completion of a new stronger sea wall in 1906, a storm in 1917 washed most of the village away, fortunately without any loss of life. You can see the remains of the village from a viewing platform just off the South West Coast Path, with information panels describing its demise.

With the onset of climate change, many locations around Britain's coasts now face the threat of coastal erosion. At-risk areas include parts of the East Anglian, Lincolnshire, Sussex and Yorkshire coasts.

RIGHT Part of the cliffside area where Hallsands was located before the 1917 storm.

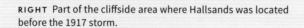

SUBMERGED PREHISTORIC REMAINS

After the last Ice Age, huge forests grew as the climate gradually warmed. Sea levels were initially much lower than today and the land extended way offshore compared with the present-day coastline. However, as sea levels rose, many forests were flooded, disappearing beneath the waves.

Remnants occasionally reappear, usually following winter storms when huge waves scour sand from beaches, and reports in the local press usually tempt visitors keen to see the forest before it disappears. Many important archaeological finds have resulted from these events, including animal

remains and raised wooden walkways, giving clues to a former way of life.

Finds in recent years have included those at Low Hauxley and Cresswell in Northumberland, Benbecula in Scotland and Portreath in Cornwall, and sites near Withernsea in Yorkshire and Silloth in Cumbria.

Often it's not long before another storm batters the coast, covering the remains with sand once more. This helps to protect them from decay, but there may be a long wait before they appear again. However, between Borth and Ynyslas in west Wales the petrified remains of a forest have become a more permanent feature since storms in 2014, at least at the time of writing.

Tree species that appear when tides are unusually low include include alder, pine, oak and birch. Dating back several thousand years, this was probably an area of fen woodland, which was then covered by peat. It is a remarkable experience to wander among these prehistoric tree trunks, some with roots still intact, where people may have passed all that time ago, and all within sight of the seaside resort of Borth, just a short way north of Aberystwyth.

Some of the UK's submerged forests date back 8,000 years or more, and there is much scientific debate about the processes by which they formed. In part their formation is due to the complexity of events since the last Ice

Age, which included periods of rising sea levels, rebound of land surfaces as the weight of the ice lifted, and prolonged wet and dry periods, some lasting centuries at a time. Waterlogging may also have occurred in peat-covered areas, which were once much more common around the coast than they are today. Finds of raised walkways provide one major clue to this past.

At Formby beach near Liverpool, there is the chance to see, at unusually low tides, the footprints of people and animals from several thousand years ago. Mammals probably included deer, wild boar and aurochs, an extinct type of wild ox. Again, sea levels were much lower then, and the prints were baked into place in the earth and mud, then filled with silt as levels rose. Check the National Trust's Formby site for more details.

LEFT Preserved tree stumps at Borth and Ynyslas, with Borth resort in the background.

CHAPTER 15

WILD WATERFALLS

See waterfalls frozen in winter or flowing backwards on a stormy day. Try to spot a spraybow in sunshine and the spectacular outflows from a reservoir following heavy rain.

Highlights

◆
See the icy tendrils of a frozen waterfall

◆
Admire the delicate patterns of a spillway flow

◆
Try to spot the beauty of a spraybow

What you might see

On a fine summer's day, a trip to a waterfall can be a great way to cool down, and following heavy rainfall the spray and power of the flow is an awe-inspiring sight. However, even more remarkable scenes await, including that of a waterfall flowing backwards in strong winds or frozen solid on a cold winter's day.

Other spectacles include underground waterfalls hidden in subterranean caves, and the beautiful and intricate patterns formed as water flows down a dam spillway following heavy rain. Photographers in particular may enjoy the challenge of trying to snap a spraybow glistening in the mist from a waterfall.

Level of difficulty ★★★★★

LOCATION sightings are surprisingly rare for some spectacles
FREQUENCY some phenomena are linked to extreme weather conditions
PREDICTABILITY difficult to predict except for a few situations
SAFETY normal outdoor risks, plus considerable risks in storm and icy conditions

....

Level ★★★ for dam spillways and show caves, Level ★★★★★ for other phenomena

OPPOSITE Mountaineer Mike Withers ice climbing in Fisher Place Gill above Thirlmere in the Lake District. This waterfall rarely comes into climbable condition but did so in the big freeze of January 2010. © Getty/Ashley Cooper

FROZEN WATERFALLS

One compensation of a harsh winter has to be the sight of a frozen waterfall, the delicate patterns of ice contrasting with the darker colours of surrounding rocks and vegetation. Ice columns may even be suspended in mid-air like stalactites in a cave. However, some flow usually remains hidden behind the ice, unless the river or stream above the falls is dry or completely frozen.

Predicting when and where frozen waterfalls will occur is difficult; once again, local news reports and social media are your best bet. Major waterfalls that have frozen in recent years include Kinder Downfall in Yorkshire, Aber Falls in Wales, Cautley Spout in Cumbria and Steall Falls in Scotland. Winter hillwalkers may be lucky enough to see smaller frozen falls on their travels, particularly in the peaks of the Lake District, Scottish Highlands and Snowdonia. Do not underestimate the risks involved: access routes may be icy or snow covered, particularly near the falls, and winter

WATERFALL SAFETY

Visits to waterfalls may range from easy walks along wide, fenced paths to steep muddy or icy scrambles requiring a good head for heights and sometimes even climbing gear. Check distance, terrain and weather forecasts before setting off, wear proper clothing and footwear, and prepare a backup plan in case of problems or delays. Indeed, stout walking boots are advisable on even the simplest routes, as paths may be wet near the falls, with steep drops alongside. One common cause of accidents is straying off paths, particularly when taking photographs or when dogs run away, while strong currents, deep water, ice and rockfalls are possible.

WATER

RIGHT An overfall spillway in full flow at Wet Sleddale Reservoir in Cumbria.

storms are another consideration. Ice climbers relish these challenges, both for the climb and the opportunity to hone their skills for visiting higher mountain regions. Expert instruction is essential before attempting this type of climbing, since it requires expertise to judge the strength of the ice before trusting your weight to it and deciding whether it is safe to proceed. Ice climbing equipment typically includes ropes, ice screws, rigid boots, crampons, a helmet and specialist axes with sharp, curving blades.

SPILLWAY FLOWS

Spillways are designed to safely discharge large volumes of water when a reservoir overflows. The resulting outflows streaming down from the crest of the dam make for a majestic sight. The air bubbles entrained into the flow often add to the spectacle, the white foam contrasting with the dam structure and surrounding hillsides.

ABOVE Bellmouth spillway at Pontsticill Reservoir. © Getty/Billy Hodgkins

The spillway at Wet Sleddale Reservoir (see pages 228–29) is an excellent example of perhaps the most common type – the overflow spillway – in which water falls steeply along a stone or concrete sloping surface to a river or stream below. Sometimes the top and bottom parts are curved to control the flow of water and reduce erosion on the spillway face and in the river bed below.

Other types of spillways include channels to the side of the dam (chute or side channel spillways) and those with a syphon arrangement. Weirs often use a free overfall spillway in which water drops straight to the river below.

While some reservoirs are remote and difficult to reach, popular spots include Burrator Reservoir on Dartmoor, the Elan Valley in Wales and Pitlochry Dam in Scotland. Older dams are often impressive structures in their own right, built from traditional stone with decorative features and towers.

Perhaps the most unusual sight of all is a bellmouth or shaft spillway, sometimes called a morning glory spillway or simply a plughole. These consist of a deep vertical column within the reservoir, with a rounded mouth over which water flows. A sloping tunnel beneath then carries the flow downstream. Examples in the UK include those at Pontsticill Reservoir in Wales and Ladybower Reservoir in the Peak District, which unusually has two spillways of this type.

Check local news reports and television bulletins for current conditions. The online reservoir situation reports published by most water companies provide additional information. As with natural waterfalls, due to the power of the flow you should only view spillways from afar, sticking to roads and public rights of way.

REVERSE FLOWS

In strong winds, another unusual waterfall sight is that of water flowing backwards, sometimes described as 'flowing in reverse' or 'uphill'. Typically, this phenomenon occurs in gale force conditions and the wind needs to be blowing towards the hillside, or at least a significant component needs to be blowing in that direction. For example, a west-facing waterfall is more likely to flow backwards in a strong westerly wind.

Given the dangers of going out in these conditions, this is one spectacle perhaps best viewed from the comfort of your own sofa. However, sometimes you might be lucky and have a chance sighting from a safe location; examples include waterfalls that flow off cliffs into the sea, such as at certain places in the Inner Hebrides, and those within sight of nearby roads.

In recent years, spectacular images of reverse flows at Kinder Downfall in the Peak District, Jenny's Lum in the Campsie Fells north of Glasgow, and Mealt Falls and Talisker Bay on the Isle of Skye have been posted online.

RIGHT A small waterfall in reverse, spotted by chance while hillwalking in the Lake District on a stormy day.

SPRAYBOWS

The incredible waterfall phenomenon that is the spraybow occurs when sunlight shines through spray to form a rainbow. Perhaps the most famous example is the mighty Victoria Falls, which straddles the Zambezi River at the border between Zambia and Zimbabwe in southern Africa. Known locally as *Mosi-oa-Tunya* ('the smoke that thunders'), after the huge amount of spray and noise it generates, the waterfall produces magnificent spraybows when the flow is high.

Spraybows also occur in the UK but are difficult to predict, given the vagaries of the weather and the fact that the sun is only high enough in the sky to produce this spectacle for part of the year. High flows are normally also required and – as with a rainbow – sightings are more likely if the sun is shining from behind you, although there are no definitive rules. Check smartphone and desktop apps favoured by landscape photographers to plan

BELOW A spraybow at Victoria Falls, viewed from the Zambian shores.

ABOVE An intermittent cascade of water in the Lake District after heavy rain.

your trip. They typically provide some combination of predictions for sun, moon and tide times, and even 3D views of how shadows and light will appear at a given location.

Waterfalls with spraybow sightings have included Aira Force in the Lake District, Henrhyd Falls and the Clydach Gorge in Wales, Hardraw Force and High Force in northern England, and the Falls of Glomach in Scotland.

Spraybows and rainbows are just two of the optical phenomena that can occur in the atmosphere. If you're lucky, you may spot the more muted arcs of fogbows, which can sometimes occur on foggy days, and broken spectres, which occur when a person's shadow is projected onto nearby mist or cloud.

OTHER UNUSUAL WATERFALLS

Intermittent waterfalls

Although waterfalls often have an air of permanence, flows can fall to a trickle in drought conditions. This has even happened at some of the world's most spectacular falls, such as at Victoria Falls, revealing the impressive cliffs normally hidden behind. On the other hand, sometimes waterfalls appear briefly where you don't expect to see them, providing an even more unusual spectacle.

One of the most remarkable events in recent years occurred at Malham Cove in Yorkshire in 2015, where a beautiful waterfall appeared for the first time in decades after heavy rainfall, causing water that would normally drain through cracks and fissures in the limestone rock to pour over the lip of the cliff face. For a short time, this was the highest single drop waterfall in England.

Like reverse waterfalls, this is a natural spectacle that is difficult to predict, so again one to plan on visiting only if you happen to see it mentioned in local news reports. Other factors that might cause waterfalls to appear suddenly include mountain lakes overflowing for the first time in years, and flows being diverted due to landslides or earthquake activity.

Underground waterfalls

Cave systems provide another place to see unusual waterfalls. These are normally the province of the potholer, but there are several you can visit if you are not an expert, including the Dan yr Ogof showcaves in south Wales and Smoo Cave in northern Scotland. Access is along well-lit walkways. More examples appear on the website of the Association of British and Irish Show Caves. But perhaps the most dramatic experience available to the public is at Gaping Gill in North Yorkshire, where local caving clubs run winch trips into the depths twice a year.

OPPOSITE A spectacular underground waterfall at Smoo Cave in northern Scotland.

HOW DO WATERFALLS FORM?

Over geological timescales, waterfalls often begin where a river or stream passes over a hard layer of rock, for example basalt situated above or upstream of softer rock such as sandstone. Over time, the softer rocks erode faster to form a cascade at first, before eventually enough rock is chipped away for the water to fall vertically into a plunge pool, forming what is often called a plunge waterfall. Sometimes the harder layer is undercut sufficiently for the resulting lip or overhang to drop off, starting the process all over again. The waterfall is said to retreat upstream to form the familiar sight of a canyon with falls at its head.

Hanging valleys are another common place to find waterfalls. These occur at the drop caused when a side valley is cut through by a glacier to be left suspended above a U-shaped main valley. Waterfalls can also form at geological fault lines caused by earthquakes.

Waterfalls are, of course, amazing places to visit even without the

promise of an unusual spectacle. Some parts of the UK have unusually high concentrations, including the Peak District, the Yorkshire Dales, the Lake District and the Scottish Highlands. Indeed, in south Wales there are so many that a region in the Brecon Beacons National park is known as Waterfall Country in tourist literature. Alternate names for falls include *linn* in Scotland, *spout* in parts of England and Scotland, and *force*, *ghyll* or *gill* in northern England.

With a drop of about 200m (656ft), the highest falls in the British Isles are often said to be Eas a' Chual Aluinn in the Scottish Highlands. Others dazzle for the volume of flow after heavy rain, such as High Force in County Durham and the Falls of Clyde in Scotland.

At a smaller scale, geological factors sometimes cause unusual effects. For example, a waterfall at St Nectan's Kieve in Cornwall passes through a hole in a rock face near the base, and double or even triple waterfalls occur in some places. At some it is even possible to walk behind the falling water, although great care must be taken on the slippery rocks.

Noss

Sumburgh Head

Marwick Head

Handa

St Kilda

Montrose Basin

Staffa

Isle of May

Loch Leven

Aberlady

Bass Rock

St Abbs Head

Islay

Lindisfarne

Farne Islands

Rathlin Island

Ailsa Craig

Coquet Island

Caerlaverock

The Gobbins

Mersehead

Campfield Marsh

Castle Espie
Strangford Lough

Mull of
Galloway

St Bees Head

Bempton Cliffs/
Flamborough Head

South Walney

Leighton Moss

Fairhaven Lake

Hoylake

Martin Mere

Donna Nook

Point of Ayr

South Stack Cliffs

Pickerings Pasture

Blakeney Point

Snettisham

Horsey Gap

Ramsey, Skomer,
Grassholm islands

Slimbridge

Two Trees Island

Cliffe Ponds

Lundy Island

Chichester
Harbour

Berry Head

Waterbirds

Seabird cities

Seals

COAST

CHAPTER 16

WHIRLING WATERBIRDS

Watch wading birds twist and turn in vast flocks as they escape the tide or a predator. See huge flocks of geese during their annual migration.

Highlights

◆
See the amazing
dance of the
dunlins

◆
Watch knot carve
out beautiful patterns
in the sky

◆
Observe huge skeins
of geese in flight

What you might see

The coastlines, estuaries and wetlands of the British Isles are home to a huge range of waterbirds, with familiar species including oystercatchers, curlews and Canada geese. While their ground-based antics are fascinating to watch, the best spectacles occur when huge numbers trace patterns in the sky, similar to the displays put on by starlings as winter approaches, with added colour and patterns. Geese flocks have their own beauty, rising as one from the ground at dawn or silhouetted against the setting sun as they return for the night.

Level of difficulty ★★★★

LOCATION typically around low-lying coastal areas, estuaries and wetlands
FREQUENCY depends on the species, but autumn to spring is often best
PREDICTABILITY challenging to predict when large numbers will take flight
SAFETY normal outdoor risks; pay particular attention to the tides

Level ★★★ for geese, Level ★★★★ for dunlin and knot displays

OPPOSITE Knot forming patterns in the sky, as they decide whether to wait out high tide at a lagoon at the RSPB Snettisham reserve.

PREVIOUS PAGES Light-bellied brent geese in flight at Strangford Lough in Northern Ireland.

WATERBIRDS: A BRIEF INTRODUCTION

From the tiny little stint to the majestic heron, wading birds of the British Isles come in all shapes and sizes. Typically seen around coastlines, estuaries and wetlands, some of the best-known species include the boisterous oystercatcher, with its carrot-like beak, the curlew, with its long, downward-curving bill, and the little egret, a beautiful white heron that has become more common in recent decades. Dunlins, knots, godwits, lapwings and redshanks can be seen feeding on mudflats at low tide, while the graceful avocet with its upturned black bill forms the RSPB logo. Some species are instantly recognisable by their call, such as the burbling cry of the curlew and the pee-wit of the lapwing. At seaside resorts, the loud piping of oystercatchers fills the air after the crowds have gone home.

Waders generally feed on the small creatures that thrive in mudflats and sandbanks. As an Environment Agency/Groundwork Mersey Valley information panel on the banks of the Mersey states: 'Mersey mud is teeming with small worms, snails and shellfish; the equivalent in calories of 5 chocolate bars, or 10 helpings of chips, in each square metre – the size of a coffee table!' For safety, different species often feed together, having no need to compete, as their bills are adapted to different types of prey.

Similarly, waterfowl are just as varied from beautifully patterned ducks, such as the wigeon and golden eye to majestic whooper and mute swans. Brent, pink-footed and barnacle geese and that 18th-century interloper, the Canada goose, are widespread. The RSPB, Wildfowl & Wetlands Trust (WWT) and Wildlife Trust websites list a wide choice of sites to view them.

As writer and broadcaster Kate Humble wrote in *Watching Waterbirds*:

> *But look a bit closer and wetlands are as bustling and busy as any city centre on a Saturday. There are birds everywhere, big ones, little ones, waddling ones, diving ones, birds that soar, birds that furiously peck the ground like manic sewing machines, and some that just hang about in groups doing not much, like bored teenagers. And once you realise how much is going on out there it is all too easy to become hooked. You can spy for hours on the comings and goings of all these birds, the scraps, the flirting, the feeding, the fighting – and then something else happens. You realise that you want to know what they all are and what they're up to out there.*

While there are plenty of opportunities to observe Britain's waterbirds, this chapter describes two two of Britain's greatest wildlife spectacles of all: the annual migrations of vast flocks of geese, and the fantastical aerial dances performed by several species of wading bird.

DANCE OF THE DUNLINS

Although many wading birds fly in flocks, some species perform a more spectacular display, in which huge numbers seem to move as one. Viewed from a distance, they trace out elegant shapes in the sky, changing from dark to light as pale undersides appear, almost disappearing when viewed head on. Strobing and rippling patterns may appear and even stripes or ovals against a darker background.

This stunning phenomenon, known as a 'wader spectacular' or murmuration, is performed by two very similar-looking species of wader, the dunlin and the knot. The knot is slightly larger and paler and, although both are fairly nondescript on the ground, they are beautiful in flight, with a white bar and brown and black markings on top of their long, tapering wings.

As Kate Humble says in *Watching Waterbirds*:

> *One of the most exciting moments I've ever had was when Chris Packham took me to see a mighty flock of knot. As they stormed over our heads in their masses, their wings whirring so loud you could hardly hear yourself speak, I had an amazing sense of the wondrous maelstroms that nature can provide – an assault on your senses and utterly breathtaking. All in all, a remarkable performance for a dumpy wader with short legs, that barely reaches the shoulder of a redshank.*

The most likely time to see this behaviour is when birds are startled into flight by the incoming tide. However, predators can also make birds take flight, with peregrine falcons in particular seeing a knot or dunlin as a tasty snack. Much as with shoaling fish, there is safety in numbers, and rapid changes in direction make it even more difficult to find a target.

Snettisham

In the UK, perhaps the best place to see wader spectaculars is at the RSPB Snettisham reserve in Norfolk. Situated on the shores of the Wash, the

reserve is set around several lagoons once used for quarrying shingle. 'Snettisham Spectaculars' usually occur between midsummer (July) and spring (April), around the highest tides of each month; check the reserve's website for specifics.

The best viewing area is on a tidal flood embankment, towards the far end of the reserve. Often the first sign of the approaching tide is when small groups of knots start flying back and forth in the distance. Then, as the tide advances, birds shuffle ever closer along the mudflats, sometimes making brief aerial hops to a better spot or heading off in small groups.

Eventually there is nowhere left to stand so the remaining birds take flight, often tracing amazing patterns in the sky. Some head inland to a favoured spot, a large lagoon behind the embankment, where two hides give great close-up views as they approach and then jostle for position after landing. Within the hides you'll find more information on the bird species that can be seen around the reserve and viewing tips for these wader spectacles.

Other locations

Further afield, dunlin and knot gather in large numbers in the Mersey, Ribble, Severn and Thames estuaries. British Trust for Ornithology surveys (see Further reading) suggest that five-year averages exceed 20,000 for each species, compared with a staggering 200,000 knots for the Wash. Nature reserves at these estuaries where you might see whirling waders include:

- **Mersey Estuary** – Pickerings Pasture (local nature reserve)
- **Ribble Estuary** – Fairhaven Lake (RSPB)
- **Severn Estuary** – Slimbridge Wetland Centre (WWT)
- **Thames Estuary** – Cliffe Pools (RSPB), Two Trees Island (Essex Wildlife Trust)

Several other estuaries see smaller concentrations of both species. One of the best known is the Dee Estuary, where displays occasionally occur on the incoming tide around Hoylake and Red Rocks on the Wirral and at the Point of Ayr in Wales. More generally, the estuary is famed for the huge numbers of birds that come ashore on extreme tides, attracting large numbers of birdwatchers.

Other destinations include the Solway Firth at Campfield Marsh (RSPB), Montrose Basin in Angus (Scottish Wildlife Trust), and the reserves at Leighton Moss (RSPB) and South Walney (Cumbria Wildlife Trust) around Morecambe Bay.

The best way to improve your chances of a sighting is to ask the experts at nature reserves or in local birdwatching groups. Failing that, unusually high tides provide a useful starting point: aim to arrive at least two to three hours before the peak to catch the incoming tide. See page 20 for tips on finding out tide times, although bird numbers on the day are, of course, another key consideration.

Due to these uncertainties, you may need to make several visits to a site before success, each time getting a better understanding of how the tides and birds behave. A good attitude to take is that you are going for an interesting day out in beautiful scenery, with any spectacle a bonus! To help you better understand the beauty of this spectacle, search online for the film *Dance of the Dunlins*, from Doray Productions in the USA.

BELOW A flock of dunlins take flight ahead of the approaching tide in the widest part of the Mersey Estuary near Pickerings Pasture, close to Liverpool. Dunlin numbers on the Mersey have exceeded 60,000 in some winters.

WATCHING GEESE AND WADING BIRDS

Waterbirds can be seen at most times of year, but numbers start building in autumn for many species as migratory birds return, staying for the winter before leaving again in spring. However, some, like terns for example, spend much of the spring and summer here.

When watching wading birds, the state of the tide is, of course, a key factor, as they often move closer to the shore as the tide comes in. High-tide roosts include nearby ponds, lagoons or wetlands. In contrast, the movement of geese is determined more by the rising and setting of the sun.

In tidally affected areas, it is always important to keep an eye on the tides to avoid getting cut off by deep, fast-flowing water. In particular, stay off mudflats, saltmarshes and sandbanks, both to avoid being trapped and disturbing waterbirds. See pages 20–22 for information on tide times and tips on water safety.

Many wildlife reserves provide hides, but elsewhere it is best to move slowly and remain below the horizon, as most birds are alert to the slightest movement. This helps to avoid startling birds into flight, which burns up valuable energy and places them at risk, particularly in colder months.

Warm clothing is usually a good idea, particularly between autumn and spring. Take a torch too if watching starlings or geese around dawn or dusk, although use it with care, as birds may be disturbed by artificial light. Many enthusiasts invest in a pair of binoculars to get a closer view. At the time of writing, avian flu has sadly impacted heavily on some waterbird populations, so please check websites before travelling to see if a reserve has been affected.

To learn more about birds, consider joining the RSPB, Wildfowl & Wetlands Trust or a Wildlife Trust whose local groups regularly organise talks and trips to birdwatching sites. Visitor centres at reserves are another good place to ask for advice and information. The international Wader Quest charity also organises talks, and an annual Wader Conservation World Watch weekend. Seabirds provide yet more birdwatching opportunities (see section starting on page 253).

The science behind aerobatic displays

In murmurations, birds fly in close formation, often making rapid twists and turns, and many theories have been advanced as to how such aerobatic feats are possible. Pioneering studies by the European Starlings in Flight

BIRDWATCHERS' CODE

The RSPB has produced a birdwatchers' code of conduct in collaboration with several other organisations. Key points include:

- Avoid disturbing birds and their habitats – the birds' interests should always come first
- Be an ambassador for birdwatching
- Know the law and the rules for visiting the countryside, and follow them
- Think about the interests of wildlife and local people before passing on news of a rare bird, especially during the breeding season

To help scientists better understand bird behaviour, the code also suggests logging sightings on BirdTrack, an easy-to-use website, or with the relevant County Bird Recorder. The full text is on the RSPB website, including a link to BirdTrack.

BELOW A murmuration of waders at the shore near Hoylake, Wirral, showing the contrast between light undersides and dark wing-tops.

(STARFLAG) project suggested that individual birds follow a simple set of rules, typically with about seven nearest neighbours but keeping clearer air ahead. Other research has suggested that air pressure variations and/or light fluctuations in the flock may be factors, due to all those flapping wings and nearby bodies.

Several research teams have reproduced starling murmurations with computer models, using mathematical representations for this behaviour. Typically, these suggest that there is no single leader and that disturbances at the edges of the flock – such as a sighting of a bird of prey – propagate inwards, making it appear to manoeuvre as one.

SPECTACULAR GEESE

While seeing a swirling mass of wading birds is hard to beat, huge flocks of geese are just as impressive a spectacle. Here it is the sight of so many large birds flying in close formation that impresses, along with the din of their honking calls and beating wings.

Perhaps the most remarkable spectacles are those of barnacle, pink-footed and brent geese. The best viewing times tend to be around first light as birds fly inland to feed, and just before dark when they return to safety offshore. Huge flocks can appear at these times, sometimes dramatically silhouetted against the rising or setting sun. However, during a full moon some geese

STARLING MURMURATIONS

Like wading birds, starlings also perform amazing aerial displays at times. Famous sites include Rome and Vancouver, and the Danes even use a special name to describe them: *sort sol*, meaning black sun. Typically, murmurations occur in late autumn and winter, with sightings any time from October to March, often peaking in December and January as more birds arrive from northern Europe.

The displays begin as birds head towards their roosts at dusk, to huddle together overnight for warmth and safety. In addition to reducing the risk from predators, this may also help to gather up stragglers during the return to the roost. Remarkably, some displays end with the flock dropping rapidly onto the roost, as if disappearing down a drain.

Timings depend on sun and cloud conditions, so the usual advice is to turn up well before sunset, in case a display begins early. If you get up early, you may even see starlings departing for the day soon after sunrise. However, as with any natural phenomenon, don't be surprised if you need to return another day for a sighting, and it is always worth checking reserve websites for the latest information.

Starling murmurations occur throughout the British Isles, except in high mountain areas. Favoured habitats include wetlands and conifer woods, and gatherings of more than a hundred thousand birds are not uncommon and sometimes exceed one million.

Nature reserves famed for their starling displays include the RSPB's reserves at Leighton Moss in Morecambe Bay, Mersehead alongside the Solway Firth, Ham Wall in Somerset and Saltholme near Middlesbrough. In the open countryside, Gretna Green is another good destination, although sites shift from year to year. Look online and you will find many more examples. Starlings are also surprisingly well adapted to life in urban areas, with well-known viewpoints including Brighton Pier, Aberystwyth Pier, Albert Bridge in Belfast, and the Runcorn area on the Mersey Estuary.

ABOVE Close formation flying during a mesmerising display of starlings at the RSPB's Leighton Moss reserve in Lancashire.

may stay out on the fields feeding by moonlight, and in stormy conditions they may also remain on land. Overnight resting places include the water, mudflats and islands, depending on the weather and the state of the tide.

Another unusual sight is that of whiffling, in which birds sometimes contort their bodies in an extraordinary way during landing, to speed up their descent. Pink-footed geese are masters of this technique, and have been filmed turning their wings and bodies almost upside down while keeping their heads virtually still, eyes facing straight ahead.

Most species migrate from higher latitudes during autumn to spend winter on these shores. They then return to their breeding grounds the following spring. These epic journeys are made to reach warmer climates and an abundance of grass, seeds, roots and other plant matter.

For barnacle geese, most of those that spend winter in the British Isles arrive from Greenland and Norway's Svalbard archipelago. You are most likely to see them in western Scotland, western Ireland and the Solway Firth. Popular reserves for barnacle geese include RSPB Loch Gruinart on the Isle of Islay and WWT Caerlaverock, RSPB Mersehead and RSPB Campfield Marsh, which are all on the shores of the Solway Firth.

Pink-footed geese also arrive from Greenland, and from Iceland and Spitsbergen. They are of a similar size to barnacle geese, but with mainly grey bodies and a pink bill, legs and feet. Perhaps the largest numbers occur at the Scottish Wildlife Trust reserve at Montrose Basin, while Caerlaverock and Mersehead are again good potential viewpoints. Others include the RSPB Snettisham reserve on the Wash, WWT Martin Mere in Lancashire and RSPB

Fairhaven Lake on the Ribble Estuary. The RSPB's Loch Leven reserve and the Aberlady Bay local nature reserve are other great Scottish destinations.

Brent geese gather in large numbers too, their location depending on the subspecies. Dark-bellied brent geese migrate from Siberia to western Europe so they tend to gather in reserves south of the Humber Estuary, including parts of the south coast of England. By contrast, light- or pale-bellied brent geese arrive from Canada and Svalbard to overwinter in Ireland and northerly locations. Well-known reserves for sightings include the WWT Castle Espie Wetland Centre in Northern Ireland, and Lindisfarne National Nature Reserve in Northumberland. Brent geese are generally smaller than barnacle and pink-footed geese, and are often said to be little larger than the Mallard ducks seen widely on lakes and ponds.

For all species, the timing of their migration south is affected by food availability and, like airline pilots, they seek out favourable winds. Arrival times therefore vary too. In flight, barnacle and pink-footed geese adopt V-shaped 'skeins' in which geese fly one behind another in formation, whereas brent geese fly in a more ragged way. The main benefit of formation flying is that following birds benefit from the updrafts from the wings of those in front. Flight times are surprisingly short: for example, pink-footed geese have been recorded reaching Scotland from Iceland in little more than a day, although some stop to refuel at the Faroe Islands.

ABOVE A flock of barnacle geese takes flight at the RSPB Mersehead reserve in Dumfries and Galloway.

A SEASONAL SENSATION AT MONTROSE BASIN

Following a migration of up to 1,200 miles pink-footed geese arrive at Montrose Basin Wildlife Reserve from mid-September, with numbers likely to peak in the middle of October.

Staff working at the Scottish Wildlife Trust's Visitor Centre, which has a superb view across the Basin, always look out for their first arrivals on the mudflats from around 13 September. Numbers will start at a few hundred and steadily work up into the thousands and then tens of thousands. On 16 October 2021, staff and volunteers counted more than 72,350 geese at the tidal mudflat.

This mass migration of hundreds of thousands of geese from Greenland and Iceland to Britain is a spectacle worth taking the time to enjoy. Visitor Centre Assistant Manager, Joanna Peaker, particularly enjoys this noisy autumn event. She enthuses:

> *It's so exciting each autumn to witness the slow but steady increase of pink-footed geese arriving in September, with numbers swelling into the middle of October.*
>
> *I would encourage everyone to take some time out and watch this key autumnal event. The sound of so many pink-footed geese on the reserve is truly breathtaking and for me marks the start of autumn.*

Pink-footed geese are best spotted on Montrose Basin at dawn and dusk.

RIGHT An imaginative digital arrivals board at the visitor centre at RSPB Fairhaven Lake for species seen in large numbers at the reserve, dunlins and pink-footed geese. © RSPB Fairhaven Lake

CHAPTER 17

SEABIRD CITIES

Walk along cliff paths or take a boat trip to see huge numbers of seabirds.
With luck, spot puffins standing guard at cliff tops or taking flight to feed.

Highlights

Watch gannets fly high above a volcanic crag	See guillemots jostle for position on a cliff face	Spot puffins standing guard on cliffs high above the sea

What you might see

Every spring, huge numbers of seabirds return to the British Isles to nest in some of the most spectacular colonies in the world. Widely known as seabird cities, these cliff-side hideouts are a hive of activity, with birds balancing side by side along ledges and outcrops.

In the air, expert aviators such as gannets and fulmars glide by on outstretched wings, while guillemots race out to sea on frantically whirring wings. With luck, you may spot the more elusive and slightly comical puffin, one of the best loved of all birds due to its large colourful beak.

Level of difficulty ★★

LOCATION typically at remote cliffs and islands
FREQUENCY the best time is often between April and July
PREDICTABILITY easy for common species but a challenge for some types
SAFETY normal outdoor risks, with particular care required around cliffs and open water

Level ★★ common types, Level ★★★ for puffins,
Level ★★★★★ for rare species

OPPOSITE Gannets soaring along cliffs at Bass Rock.

BRITISH SEABIRDS

Every spring, huge numbers of seabirds return to the British Isles. Some, like gannets, are masters of the air, soaring high above the cliffs. Others, like guillemots and puffins, dart back and forth hunting for food, their wings moving almost too fast to see.

Their favoured nesting spots are rocky cliffs and headlands, often in spectacular locations. At the busiest sites, every ledge seems to be occupied as birds jostle for position. These amazing places are widely known as seabird cities.

One of the smallest and most common species is the guillemot, easily recognised by its smart brown-black and white plumage. With no nests, eggs are laid directly on rock or soil and are much narrower at one end, perhaps to help prevent them rolling off into the sea.

The slightly larger razorbill is usually found nearby, its stockier build, darker feathers and heavier white-striped bill the main distinguishing features. While guillemots rely on sheer numbers for protection, razorbills prefer to hide away in smaller groups, often under overhanging ledges.

Kittiwakes, with a white body and pale grey wings, are another commonly seen species. They belong to the gull family but have a more elegant shape. Unlike guillemots, they build nests, often balanced on ledges and outcrops. Unusually for seabirds, some raise chicks inland, most famously the Tyne Kittiwakes, which nest on bridges and buildings along the shores of the River Tyne in Newcastle and Gateshead.

The largest species seen around Britain is the gannet. Noted for its beautiful yellow head colouration, with long, elegant black-tipped wings and a wingspan of up to around 2m (6.6ft), these magnificent birds are able to stay aloft for hours. Adults are sometimes seen returning from sea with seaweed in their bills, an important construction material for their nests. Chicks typically start hatching in June and most leave the nest by August or September, their first flights a daring dive into the sea.

Like the gannet, fulmars have long, narrow wings optimised for long-distance flight. Only slightly smaller, they have a white body and speckled grey upper wings. When nesting, one of their defences is to spit a foul-smelling jet of sticky fish oil at predators and intruders. Occasionally this surprises rock climbers, who accidentally stumble across a nest outside areas closed for nesting restrictions.

Other common British seabirds include cormorants and the slightly smaller shag. With mainly black feathers and a hooked beak, both are instantly recognisable, although difficult to tell apart unless side by side or when a male shag displays its quiff of feathers in spring. Experts, of course,

ABOVE A guillemot takes flight at the RSPB St Bees Head reserve, with a chick visible on the ledge above.

use a range of other subtle distinguishing features. Sightings inland are most likely to be of cormorants, which are one of the few seabirds to have adapted to fishing along rivers, canals and lakes. This is where you are most likely to see the classic image of a cormorant perched on the shore, drying outstretched wings.

Of the common British seabirds, the comical looking puffins are perhaps best loved. However, they can be difficult to spot because they typically nest in burrows on top of islands and headlands. Other well-known seabirds include the various species of terns and gulls, of which the artic tern and herring gull are perhaps the most familiar. Famously, there is no such thing as a seagull; in fact, the gull (*Laridae*) family encompasses many species, including the black-headed gull and the great black-backed gull.

VISITING A SEABIRD CITY

Nesting seabirds are one of the easier types of bird to see, and for two to three months each year you have a good chance of a sighting if you visit the right place. However, it may take several trips before you experience classic sights, such as a puffin with a beak full of sand eels or a gannet diving nearby. This uncertainty is one of the joys of a visit, in addition to the overall spectacle. If you're just starting out, the easiest place to begin is at a nature reserve or on a guided boat trip: check reserve websites for the best times of year to visit. Remember to take a pair of binoculars or a telephoto lens if you want a close-up view.

Larger sites often have visitor centres with all the latest information and usually a café and shop too. Look out for a whiteboard with the latest sightings. However, at smaller sites or outside normal working hours, you will need to find your own way, so it is worth doing some online research first, for example on RSPB and Wildlife Trust blog posts and social media feeds.

If you have only ever visited reserves inland, you'll find that one surprising feature of seabird reserves is that many have clifftop viewing platforms. These provide a fabulous view but sometimes require a good head for heights. Cliffs can be much cooler and windier than inland, so an extra layer or two helps, along with appropriate footwear for walking on rough, potentially slippery paths. Given the proximity to steep drops,

BELOW Razorbills on an outcrop at the RSPB Bempton Cliffs reserve.

children and dogs should be kept well away.

Boat trips usually have the advantage of an expert guide to point out highlights along the way. If you are lucky, you may even spot seals, porpoises or dolphins. Some boat operators offer landings, although usually with restrictions due to the protected nature of many reserves. As with clifftop visits, it is worth wrapping up warm and taking waterproofs in case of rain or spray. Many trips are seasonal, so check operator's websites first before travelling.

Beyond reserves, there is always a chance of seeing seabirds on clifftop walks. From a distance, one clue is often a white streaking to the cliff face caused by bird droppings, known as guano – once prized as a natural fertiliser. As you get closer, lines of guillemots may become visible on ledges, or gannets soaring high overhead, the cacophony of bird cries another possible clue.

If you develop a taste for birdwatching, look out for rarer coastal residents, such as white-tailed eagles, which are often called sea eagles. Spring can also be a good time to see wading birds (see the chapter on Whirling Waterbirds for ideas of places to visit). To learn more, the British Trust for Ornithology (BTO) and Joint Nature Conservation Committee (JNCC) websites are a mine of information. The RSPB website lists many other reserves too, beyond the examples in this chapter.

As with waterbirds, following the guidance in the Birdwatchers' Code of Conduct (see page 246) helps to prevent distress to these increasingly rare species. Avian flu has also impacted heavily on some seabird populations, so please check websites first to see if a reserve has been affected.

BIRD'S EYE VIEW

With their beautiful coastal scenery, many clifftop nature reserves are worth visiting for the walk alone. However, seabirds introduce a sense of wonder that catches many first-time visitors by surprise.

Bempton Cliffs

For sheer numbers and variety, the RSPB's Bempton Cliffs reserve in Yorkshire is one of the most impressive. The chalk cliffs here rise 400ft above the sea, and during the height of season (April to July), species include gannets, guillemots, razorbills, fulmars, shags, herring gulls, kittiwakes and puffins. The experience has been described by the RSPB as 'life on the edge – the sights, sounds and smells of soaring and swooping seabirds combined with panoramic sea views is unforgettable.'

Six viewing platforms lie alongside the clifftop trails, the southernmost looking out towards a sea stack, often with rows of nesting birds along its ledges. Others give a closer view, such as of kittiwakes or guillemots and gannets and fulmars soaring in the sea air. Occasionally there are rarer visitors, most notably a black-browed albatross that first appeared in 2017 and then returned several times since, having made the Baltic Sea its home after straying off course from the south Atlantic.

The reserve has a visitor centre, café and shop and is near Bridlington, from where it can also be visited aboard the *Yorkshire Belle* pleasure cruiser. These trips pass Flamborough Head, which is another renowned seabird nesting site, managed by the Yorkshire Wildlife Trust.

St Bees Head

To the west, the delicate reds and creams of sandstone await at St Bees Head in Cumbria. These are the highest cliffs in northwest England and the site of another RSPB reserve, again with spectacular viewing platforms. The walk begins at the seaside resort of St Bees along a steep and at times rocky path

WHAT IS A SEABIRD?

A characteristic feature of seabirds is that they spend much of their lives at sea, only coming ashore to breed. Most are adapted for the harsh marine environment, with closely layered feathers for water resistance and a thick layer of fat for insulation.

Internationally, there are more than 400 species, including albatrosses, penguins, frigate birds and pelicans. About 25 of these regularly breed in Britain and Ireland. Full names – rather than the colloquial names used in this chapter – include the Atlantic puffin, black-legged kittiwake, northern fulmar, northern gannet, European shag, European and Leach's storm petrel, and the Arctic skua.

At up to 3.5m (11.5ft), the wandering albatross has the greatest wingspan, and is part of an order called tubenoses (*Procellariiformes*), which include fulmars and the tiny storm petrel. Albatrosses spend much of their life on the wing, and are to ride the updrafts from waves over huge distances.

Guillemots, razorbills and puffins belong to the strangely named auk family. This once included the great auk, which became extinct in the 19th century. At some sites you might spot the rarer black guillemot or a bridle guillemot, which has a white ring around the eye and a white line behind it.

Typical seabird diets include fish and crustaceans. Some scavenge too, perhaps most notoriously the herring gull, which has raided many a diner's

close to the cliff edge.

The star visitors here are guillemots, including nesting black guillemots, some of just a few in England. Other species include kittiwakes, razorbills, fulmars and cormorants. The path continues beyond the reserve to pass St Bees Lighthouse, with good views north towards Whitehaven and along the Cumbrian coast.

Other locations

Other popular RSPB seabird sites include South Stack Cliffs on Anglesey and the Mull of Galloway in Dumfries and Galloway. At South Stack, Ellin's Tower looks out on the cliffs, and the long line of steps leading down to the lighthouse provides another fabulous viewpoint. The Mull of Galloway is the southernmost point in Scotland and a good viewpoint for the occasional passing dolphin or porpoise too. Lighthouse tours and a clifftop café add to the experience.

fish and chips at seaside resorts. The puffin's favoured catch is sand eels, leading to the classic photograph of a bird with its beak full of this silvery fish.

Some seabirds dive for their prey. Cormorants are masters at diving, sometimes spending minutes under water before bobbing up again far away, while guillemots are capable of reaching depths of several hundred feet. By contrast, the albatross is mainly a surface feeder, as are kittiwakes and fulmars.

Gannets take things a stage further by diving from on high, dramatically pulling back their wings as they enter the water. Impact speeds can exceed 100km/h (about 60mph) and provide both an element of surprise and the chance to catch fast-moving prey. Air sacs in the skull act like airbags and bony tissues as a crash helmet to absorb the massive impact forces. Other adaptations help to protect the eyes and nostrils. During the breeding season, some gannets fly more than 100km (62 miles) from their nests in search of fish.

Threats to seabirds include overfishing of food sources, avian flu, accidental catches in fishing gear, predators at nesting sites and declining fish populations. British species that appear on the UK's 'Birds of Conservation Concern' Red List include kittiwakes, shags and puffins. These risks highlight the importance of the work of the RSPB, WWT, Wildlife Trusts and other conservation organisations.

Around the coast, there are many other chances to see seabirds in the breeding season, although not always in such huge numbers. For example, at St Abb's Head National Nature Reserve in Scotland, you can sometimes spot guillemots and kittiwakes from a spectacular coastal walk. This begins near the picturesque fishing harbour of St Abbs and leads to a lighthouse, another great viewpoint.

Almost 500 miles away, Berry Head in Devon has the largest colony of guillemots on the south coast of England. Smaller numbers of fulmars, kittiwakes, cormorants and shags sometimes appear too. A hide near the visitor centre and café provides distant views of the cliffs and lies close to the well-preserved walls of a Napoleonic fort. The guillemots here are sometimes jokingly called 'Brixham Penguins', after the nearby town of that name.

If you take a ferry trip from the mainland, you'll be able to visit Lundy Island in the Bristol Channel, Marwick Head in Orkney and Sumburgh Head in the Shetland Islands. Similarly, the paths around the RSPB's West Light Seabird Centre are a well-known place to see seabirds on Rathlin Island in Northern Ireland.

However, for perhaps the most vertiginous views of all, the Gobbins in Northern Ireland are difficult to beat. Here, expert guides take visitors along spectacular cliff-face paths on Islandmagee. Nesting seabirds can include guillemots, razorbills, kittiwakes and puffins.

ABOVE Massed ranks of guillemots at the RSPB South Stack Cliffs reserve.

OPPOSITE Gannets, guillemots and kittiwakes nesting on a sea stack, seen from a viewing platform at the RSPB Bempton Cliffs reserve.

BOAT TRIPS

Although clifftop sites have many attractions, a boat trip gives you the chance of a closer view, often with a knowledgeable guide to describe the sights along the way.

Bass Rock

Perhaps the most famous destination by boat is Bass Rock, a spectacular volcanic plug with cliffs rising more than 100m (328ft) out of the Firth of Forth. It has the largest seabird breeding population in Britain, ahead of other Scottish hideouts such as St Kilda and Ailsa Craig.

The first gannets usually appear well before reaching the rock, flying low over the water or passing overhead. Before long, you realise that the whiteness on the cliffs is a multitude of birds, seemingly perched on every available ledge. Thousands also nest at the shallower southern end of the island around Bass Rock Lighthouse.

The Scotland Seabird Centre and Sula Boat Trips operate trips from North Berwick, often passing Craigleith island on the way, another seabird

haven. Many people visit the seabird centre too, which is a great place to learn more about wildlife and conservation, and see live webcam feeds from Bass Rock, Craigleith and the Isle of May. Boats for the Isle of May leave from both North Berwick and Anstruther, on the opposite shore of the Firth of Forth.

Other Scottish destinations include Handa (Scottish Wildlife Trust), Ailsa Craig and the Noss National Nature Reserve in Shetland.

Other destinations

In Wales, popular wildlife watching trips include those to Ramsey Island and the more distant islands of Skomer and Grassholm. Trips depart from St Justinians, just a short way from the city of St Davids in Pembrokeshire. This is close to the site of The Bitches tidal race, as described on pages 134–35.

In Northumberland, the Farne Islands and Coquet Island are other superb destinations; see the National Trust and RSPB websites for links to boat operators.

BELOW A gannet approaches cliffs at Bass Rock.

GROUND NESTING AND BURROWING SEABIRDS

While many seabirds nest on cliffs, some choose grassy areas nearby to bring up their chicks. The best known is the puffin, which often takes advantage of disused rabbit burrows. If all else fails, puffins are also known to nest under overhangs or in cavities in cliff faces. Adults normally mate for life, raising a single chick each year known as a puffling.

When visiting a site by boat, you may therefore see surprisingly few puffins, even if you know there are many there. Sometimes, the most visible are those seeming to stand guard at clifftop edges. However, when ashore, birds may land nearby if you sit quietly near a cliff edge because you are seen as protection from the greater threat of great black-backed gulls. At times, you may see huge rafts of puffins sheltering offshore, especially early in the breeding season. Islands famous for large numbers of puffins include Staffa and the Isle of May in Scotland, Skomer in Wales, the Farne Islands and Coquet Island in England, and Rathlin Island in Northern Ireland. Shetland and Orkney also have large populations.

BELOW A puffin taking flight near the Isle of May in Scotland.

OPPOSITE A puffin watching visitors on the Isle of Staffa.

Other ground nesting birds include Manx shearwaters and European storm petrels. However, as they emerge mainly at night, they are most usually seen when flying offshore. Manx shearwaters have long black-topped wings, suitable for long-distance migration, and storm petrels are one of the smallest seabirds, with a more energetic flight pattern.

Terns typically build their nests on or near shingle beaches. In flight, they are one of the most beautiful seabirds, with long, finely patterned wings and – in most species – an elegant black-capped head. Those most common to Britain are the arctic, common, little and sandwich terns. They are one of the world's great long-distance travellers, and arctic terns from the UK have been recorded as far afield as South Africa and Antarctica on their annual migrations.

Compared with cliff-nesting birds, ground-nesting species risk predation from rats, which is why remote islands are often favoured. In recent decades, several puffin populations have been almost wiped out due to accidental introductions. However, thanks to conservation work, some have now recovered, including at Lundy Island in England, and Ramsey Island and Puffin Island in Wales.

CHAPTER 18

SEAL PUPS

See fluffy white grey seal pups during autumn and early winter and adults year round. Try to spot more elusive harbour seal pups during the summer.

Highlights

◆
See fluffy white seal pups soon after they are born

◆
Enjoy watching curious adults bobbing up to see you

◆
Watch beachmaster males patrolling their territory

What you might see

Grey seal pups are some of the most endearing animals seen around our shores, their large black eyes peering out from a furry white coat. Sightings are often in remote rocky bays around cliffs and islands, making the trip to see them an adventure in itself. However, some seals choose sandy beaches to raise their young, hidden away behind sand dunes. Once weaned, they soon leave the safety of dry land for the water, joining adults to venture more widely, and can often be spotted resting on sandbanks or bobbing up to watch spectators nearby.

The pups of the UK's other main seal species – the harbour seal – swim from birth, making them more difficult to distinguish from the adults.

Level of difficulty ★★

LOCATION typically around remote rocky bays but on beaches too
FREQUENCY pupping occurs mainly in summer or early winter, depending on the species
PREDICTABILITY very dependent on the site and numbers vary annually
SAFETY normal outdoor risks, although be aware that adult seals are dangerous

....

Level ★★ for grey seal pups, Level ★★★★ for harbour seal pups

OPPOSITE A grey seal pup and mother.

ATLANTIC GREY SEAL

The Atlantic grey seal is one of the largest mammals in the British Isles. Mature adult bulls can weigh 300kg (661lb) and exceed 2m (6.6ft) from snout to tail. Along with the common or harbour seal, the Atlantic grey is one of two species of seal found around our shores. The Latin name – *Halichoerus grypus* – translates as hook-nosed sea pig.

It is grey seal pups that most visitors hope to see. These are at their most endearing for the first two to three weeks after birth, and they bear their furry white coat until weaned. At breeding colonies, it can be amazing to see so many seals together, with females caring for their young and larger male 'bull' seals patrolling their harem. Breeding often takes place on remote rocky shores, requiring a boat trip or cliffside walk for a sighting, which is all part of the adventure. However, some seal colonies favour beaches hidden away behind sand dunes, which act as a refuge during storms.

The following whistlestop tour lists some of the most accessible pupping sites around the British Isles, and the websites of the Wildlife Trusts, RSPB and tourist boards are good places to search for more. Of course, adult grey seals are interesting to watch too, with a much better chance of a sighting, and during the tourist season you can often find boat trips from seaside resorts. Other highlights on a trip can include spotting nesting seabirds, wading birds, dolphins and porpoises.

BELOW A grey seal pup at Donna Nook National Nature Reserve.

ABOVE Grey seal pup and adults at Donna Nook National Nature Reserve.

East and northeast England

Perhaps surprisingly, the low-lying shores of Lincolnshire and Norfolk see some of the largest numbers of seal pups. The Donna Nook National Nature Reserve is perhaps the best known. Here, the main pupping season takes place in November and December on an extensive area of mudflats and intertidal channels hidden away behind sand dunes. The Lincolnshire Wildlife Trust sets up a fenced-off seal viewing area and has a weekly seal 'pupdate' on their website.

Further south, at Blakeney Point in Norfolk, the main pupping season is again typically in November and December. The National Trust website gives links to boat operators, but double-check for winter schedules. Visits are also popular in summer to see grey and common adult seals hauled out on the sand and shingle of this remote peninsula. Further around the coast, volunteer wardens from the Friends of Horsey Seals help to protect seals at the beaches at Horsey and Winterton, another important pupping location.

To the north, the Farne Islands in Northumberland are a very different type of destination. Here, seals raise pups on a string of uninhabited islands, using rocky ledges and bays for shelter, with higher points for escape during storms. The National Trust website again gives links to boat operators.

ABOVE Juvenile seal pup viewed during the breeding season in November.

Additional sights include the spectacular lighthouses on the islands and distant views of Bamburgh Castle. In spring and early summer, the islands are a great place to see puffins and other seabirds.

Scotland

To the north, St Abb's Head and the Isle of May see perhaps the largest breeding colonies along the east coast of Scotland. It is in the north and west though, that the most dramatic numbers occur. Here, just two locations – northern Orkney and the Monach Islands – account for almost a third of all pups born in the British Isles. Several other large colonies gather in remote islands and bays, from the Firth of Clyde to the Shetland Isles. However, access is more challenging, as most tour boat operators have already finished for the winter by the time seal pupping starts. Visitors therefore often need to make their own arrangements.

Elsewhere

Further south, the other main breeding colonies are in northwest England and Pembrokeshire. At the South Walney Nature Reserve in Cumbria, seals haul out on a remote shingle beach to breed, and adults are sometimes spotted swimming near the shore at high tide. A 'seal cam' streams close-up images to the visitor centre and the Cumbria Wildlife Trust's website.

Apart from isolated spots, there are then no major breeding sites until Pembrokeshire, where the many rocky bays and remote islands are much favoured. Ramsey and Skomer islands are particular hotspots. Smaller numbers are found in north Wales, Devon, Cornwall, Lundy Island, the Isles of Scilly, and Rathlin Island in Northern Ireland. Of course, adults can also be seen at many of these locations at other times.

Watching seals

When watching seals, it is important to look out for their welfare and your own safety. Adult seals are formidable beasts with sharp teeth, and bulls can move surprisingly quickly across the ground. Typical advice is to keep quiet and well away. Don't attempt to feed, approach or touch them. Also, don't get between a seal and its pup or the sea. Dogs, in particular, should be left at home, as even barking can disturb seals.

Signs of alarm include hissing noises, heads turning to look at you, raised flippers and returning to the water. If startled, a frightened seal may injure itself on rocks and stones, with a pup's survival threatened if the bond with its mother is broken.

Information panels are usually available at the more popular sites along with warning signs describing local rules and regulations. The website of the Seal Protection Action Group is also worth exploring before making a trip. The UK government website notes that 'it is an offence to intentionally or recklessly kill, injure or take a seal'.

A year in the life of a grey seal

Grey seals have one of the most remarkable life cycles of any British mammal. The annual breeding season begins in autumn, as heavily pregnant cows come ashore to give birth and the strongest bulls – known as beachmasters –

THE SELKIE FOLK

Many stories surround seals, or selkies, as they are known in the myths and legends of the northern isles of Scotland. Some may arise from the long, plaintive wail that grey seals make when resting out of the water. According to folklore, selkies are seals that shed their skins and change to human form on land and are often of handsome or beautiful appearance. Tales abound of elopements with selkie lovers, selkie children with webbed feet and hands, and unscrupulous rogues stealing or hiding female selkie's skins. Several famous singers, including Joan Baez and June Tabor, have recorded versions of 'The Great Silkie of Sule Skerry', a traditional Shetland and Orkney ballad.

compete to build up a harem of potential mates for when the pups are weaned.

The first arrivals are normally in southwest England during August or September. They then extend through October or November in Scotland and only really get underway in November on the east coast of England. Dates vary, depending on recent weather and the extent to which adults have been able to build up a store of energy-rich blubber over the summer for the trials ahead.

The breeding colony is called a rookery and traditional sites include shingle and rocky beaches, with higher ground nearby for shelter during storms. Sandy beaches with dunes for escape are also attractive, as there is less risk of pups being injured on rocks. Although clumsy looking on land, grey seals are able to climb a surprisingly long way from the shore.

The females give birth soon after arrival and normally only have one pup. The pup's coats are initially stained yellow from the amniotic fluid that surrounds the embryo, but this soon disappears and they gain their appealing white colour.

Suckling typically continues for two to three weeks, with pups rapidly gaining weight on the rich fatty milk that is more than half fat. This high-calorie diet is equivalent to about 20,000 calories a day; in comparison, even a top weightlifter only consumes a few thousand calories a day before a crucial competition. Pups typically gain about 2kg (4.4lb) a day, reaching a weight of 40–50kg (88–110lb) when weaned. The mother does not feed during this time and can lose up to half her body weight.

Once lactation ends, a female's priority is to return to the sea to feed and to mate, as she is now in season. As the gestation period is about eight to nine months, the fertilised egg initially remains in suspension, before implanting into the womb – this means that pups are ready for birth at about the same time again the following year. Bulls likewise do not feed while onshore and often stay until the last mating possibility has passed. Being a beachmaster is a full-time job.

Once weaned, pups shed their fur coat, which is replaced by a dark grey or black mottled denser coat that is fully waterproof. Most can swim from birth but usually do not enter the water unless they have to, as the blubber and new coat are essential for warmth. The markings on their coats are unique, which is a great boon to marine researchers in tracking their progress. After the mother leaves, pups can live off blubber alone for up to a month or so but must then head off to sea to learn to hunt.

At sea, grey seals are great travellers, known to swim 100km (62 miles) or more a day. Adults are able to dive to depths of more than 200m (650ft) and remain underwater for half an hour. Prey includes fish and crustaceans. Most spend more than half their lives at sea, although regularly 'haul out' for rest,

ADVENTURES IN SEAL TRAVEL

Grey seals and common seals can be seen in the most surprising places, and some more unusual haul-out sites include pontoons in harbours and sandbanks in estuaries. For example, sightings are fairly common in Granton Harbour in Edinburgh and near Liverpool on the Mersey Estuary.

Seals even chase fish into rivers and some have made the local news as they pass by. Sightings in recent years have occurred at the River Eden in Cumbria, the River Severn in Worcestershire, and the Great Ouse in Norfolk. Tidal bores occur in all of these estuaries, but it is perhaps a step too far to say this is a factor; however, they do all have unusually large tidal ranges.

ABOVE An inquisitive adult grey seal watching the antics of spectators on the shore near the disused lifeboat station on Hilbre Island, at the mouth of the Dee Estuary.

The Mersey seals have probably swum around from the nearby Dee Estuary, where in summer several hundred haul out onto sandbanks at low tide. Individuals occasionally reach Warrington, about 32km (20 miles) upstream from Liverpool, where they briefly become local celebrities until they return to sea again. In autumn, much of the Dee Estuary population heads to the west coast of Wales, where the rocky shores are more conducive to raising pups.

particularly during the spring moulting season.

Male seals are typically able to mate from about four to six years old, reaching sexual maturity at about ten years. They tend to live for around 25 years, while females reach sexual maturity sooner and live about ten years longer. In the first year, pup mortality rates sometimes exceed 50%. Threats include infection, hunger, pollution, fishing nets, storms, and disturbances from people and dogs.

Internationally, grey seals are one of the rarest seal species and a remarkable 40% or so are found around the British Isles. The Atlantic grey seal is one of three subspecies, with a range from Iceland to the Barents Sea and to northern France.

COMMON (HARBOUR) SEALS

Common or harbour seals are the other main species of seal found around British shores. Like grey seals, they are classed as true seals (*Phocidae*), since they have no ear flaps, unlike a sea lion say, which is classed as an eared seal. There are 19 species of true seal worldwide.

Perhaps 40,000 to 50,000 common seals live around the British Isles, which is less than half the population of grey seals. Outside the breeding season, the two species are often found together on haul-out sites with no obvious rivalry. When in the distance or covered with mud, the species can be quite hard to tell apart. However, one distinguishing feature is that the

OPPOSITE Common (harbour) seals at Chichester Harbour in Sussex, one of the most southerly places for sightings in the British Isles. Both grey and common seals haul out on mudflats in secluded creeks, like those around Thorney Island. Seal watching boat trips depart from Itchenor Jetty.

ABOVE Common seals hauled out at Cloghy Rocks Nature Reserve in the Narrows at Strangford Lough, a channel with a strong tidal race as tides rise and fall.

common seal has V-shaped nostrils, rather than the almost parallel nostrils of a grey seal. Their eyes also face more directly forwards which, combined with their more pronounced forehead, means that their facial appearance is sometimes said to resemble that of a cat. Grey seals have a more pronounced muzzle and eyes more to the side.

Common seals are generally smaller than grey seals, with adult males reaching lengths and weights of up to about 2m (6.6ft) and 130kg (287lb). They are generally lighter in colour, but this is not a reliable indicator as some grey seals are also various shades of light brown during the year.

The main difference between the two species is during breeding, as common seal pups normally head into the water soon after birth. Typically, they are born on tidally affected sandbanks or beaches, allowing them to swim off on the next tide. They then feed on their mother's milk until weaned, hauling out to rest when required. At birth, they already have a sleek, dark mottled waterproof coat and are therefore harder to distinguish from adults, particularly once they have put on a few kilograms. The breeding season is typically earlier in the year than for grey seals, during June and July.

Common seals are widely found around the British Isles, particularly in the Scottish Isles and, to a lesser extent, around the Wash in East Anglia, and Strangford Lough in Northern Ireland. Similar safety considerations apply for watching common seals as for grey seals, as described under 'Watching seals' on page 271.

APPENDICES

FURTHER READING

Books, reports and scientific papers

METEOR SHOWERS

Dunlop, Storm and Tirion, Wil, *2023 Guide to the Night Sky: A Month-By-Month Guide to Exploring the Skies Above Britain and Ireland* (Collins, 2022)

Francis-Baker, Tiffany, *The Dark Skies of Britain & Ireland: A Stargazer's Guide* (Bradt, 2021)

Lunsford, Robert, *Meteors and How to Observe Them* (*Astronomers' Observing Guides*) (Springer, 2009)

Smith, Caroline, Russell, Sara and Almeida, Natasha, *Meteorites: The Story of Our Solar System*, 2nd edition (Firefly Books, 2019)

ECLIPSES AND SUPERMOONS

Anderson, Jay, 'The Enchantment of Eclipses', *Weather*: 54(7), 202–7 (Special Issue: Eclipses), 2012 (first published 1999)

Dunlop, Storm and Tirion, Wil, *Night Sky Almanac 2023: a Stargazer's Guide* (Collins, 2022)

Kerss, Tom, *Moongazing: Beginner's Guide to Exploring the Moon* (Collins, 2018)

Littmann, Mark, Espenak, Fred and Willcox, Ken, *Totality: Eclipses of the Sun*, 3rd edition (Oxford University Press, 2009)

OPPOSITE Guillemots and a fulmar at RSPB Marwick Head, one of the best seabird sites in the Orkney Islands.

NORTHERN LIGHTS

Case, NA, Marple et al. 'AuroraWatch UK: An Automated Aurora Alert System', *Earth and Space Science*: 4(12), 746–54, 2017

Green, Lucie, *15 Million Degrees: A Journey to the Centre of the Sun* (Penguin, 2017)

Kerss, Tom, *Northern Lights: The Definitive Guide to Auroras* (Collins, 2021)

Stimac, Valerie, *Lonely Planet Dark Skies: A Practical Guide to Astrotourism* (Lonely Planet, 2019)

HIDDEN CURRENTS

Dunlop, Storm, *Weather: A Very Short Introduction* (Oxford University Press, 2017)

Hamblyn, Richard, in association with the Met Office, *The Cloud Book: How to Understand the Skies* (David & Charles, 2008)

Met Office, *Very British Weather: Over 365 Hidden Wonders from the World's Greatest Forecasters* (Ebury Press, 2020)

Watts, Alan, *Instant Storm Forecasting* (Bloomsbury, 2009)

MOUNTAIN CLOUDS

Anderson, Fletcher, *Flying the Mountains: A Training Manual For Flying Single-Engine Aircraft* (McGraw Hill, 2003)

Clement, Jean-Marie, *Dancing with the Wind* (Topfly, 2015)

Pedgley, David, *Mountain Weather*, 3rd edition (Cicerone, 2006)

Wallington, CE, *Meteorology for Glider Pilots*, 3rd edition (John Murray, 1977)

NAMED WINDS AND WEATHER

Discovering Britain, *Troublesome wind: a self-guided walk in the North Pennines* (Royal Geographical Society with IBG, 2013)

Hunt, Nick, *Where the Wild Winds Are: Walking Europe's Winds From the Pennines to Provence* (Nicholas Brealey Publishing, 2017)

Uttley, David, *The Anatomy of the Helm Wind: The Scourge of the Cumbrian East Fellside* (Bookcase, 1998)

Veale, Lucy and Endfield, Georgina, 'The Helm Wind of Cross Fell', *Weather*: 69(1), 3–7, 2014

TIDAL BORES

Bowers, DG and Roberts, EM, *Tides: a Very Short Introduction* (Oxford University Press, 2019)

Chanson, Hubert, *Tidal Bores, Aegir, Eagre, Mascaret, Pororoca: Theory and Observations* (World Scientific Publishing, 2012)

Colas, Antony, *Mascaret: Prodige de la Marée* (Yep Editions, 2017)

Sene, Kevin, *Tidal Bores of England, Scotland and Wales* (Troubador, 2021)

TIDAL RACES

Aldersey-Williams, Hugh, *Tide: The Science and Lore of the Greatest Force on Earth* (Penguin Books, 2017)

Endean, Ken, *Coastal Turmoil: Winds, Waves and Tidal Races* (Bloomsbury, 2010)

Pike, Dag, 'The UK's 11 Fiercest Tide Races', *Yachting Monthly*, 18 December 2020

Thomson, W, *The Book of Tides* (Quercus Editions, 2016)

LOW TIDE WALKS

Caton, Peter, *No Boat Required: Exploring Tidal Islands*, 2nd edition (Troubador, 2022)

Drewe, Lisa, *Islandeering: Adventures Around the Edge of Britain's Hidden Islands* (Wild Things, 2019)

Naldrett, Peter, *Treasured Islands: The Explorer's Guide to Over 200 of the Most Beautiful and Intriguing Islands Around Britain* (Conway, 2021)

Robinson, Cedric, *Time and Tide – 50 Golden Years on Morecambe Bay* (Great Northern Books, 2013)

AUTUMN COLOURS

Aas, G and Riedmiller, A, *Trees of Britain & Europe* (Collins Nature Guide, 2013)

Allan, Vicky and Deacon, Anna, *For the Love of Trees: A Celebration of People and Trees* (Black and White Publishing, 2021)

Toomer, Simon, *50 Great Trees of the National Trust* (The National Trust, 2022)

Woodland Trust, The, *State of the UK's Woods and Trees 2021* (The Woodland Trust, 2021)

WILDFLOWER DISPLAYS

Gibbons, Bob, *Wildflower Wonders: the 50 Best Wildflower Sites in the World* (Bloomsbury, 2011)

Harrap, Simon, *Harrap's Wildflowers: a Field Guide to the Wild Flowers of Britain & Ireland* (Bloomsbury, 2018)

Pilgrim, Emma and Hutchinson, Nicola, *Bluebells for Britain: A Report on the 2003 Bluebells for Britain Survey* (Plantlife, 2004)

Raven, Sarah, *Wild Flowers* (Bloomsbury, 2011)

RUTTING DEER

British Deer Society, *Wild Deer of the UK*, six leaflets on deer species (The British Deer Society, 2022)

King, Simon, *Nature Watch: how to track and observe wildlife* (Quadrille Publishing, 2016)

Pemberton, JM and Kruuk, LEB, *Red deer research on the Isle of Rum NNR: Management Implications*, NatureScot (Scottish Natural Heritage, 2015)

Taylor, Marianne, *RSPB British Naturefinder* (Bloomsbury, 2018)

SALMON RUNS

Falkus, H, *Salmon Fishing: A Practical Guide* (Cengage Learning, 1980)

Hendry, K and Cragg-Hine, D, *Ecology of the Atlantic Salmon* (Natural England, 2003)

Jones, PD, 'From Water Quality and Fisheries in the Mersey Estuary, England: A Historical Perspective', *Marine Pollution Bulletin*: 53(1–4), 144–54, 2006

Wigan, Michael, *The Salmon: The Extraordinary Story of the King of Fish* (William Collins, 2014)

SUNKEN VILLAGES AND WILD WATERFALLS

Arthur, Lina, *Snow and Ice: Winter Mountaineering Routes of Great Britain* (The Oxford Alpine Club, 2021)

Crow, Vivienne, *Walks to Waterfalls: Walks to Cumbria's Best Waterfalls (Lake District Top 10 Walks)* (Northern Eye Books, 2012)

Naldrett, Peter, *Days Out Underground: 50 Subterranean Adventures Beneath Britain* (Bloomsbury, 2019)

Roberts, Gordon, *The Lost World of Formby Point: Footprints on the Prehistoric Landscape 5000BC to 100BC* (Alt Press, 2014)

WHIRLING WATERBIRDS

Frost, TM, Calbrade, NA, Birtles, GA et al., *Waterbirds in the UK 2019/20: The Wetland Bird Survey* (British Trust for Ornithology, 2021)

Holden, Peter and Cleeves, Tim, *RSPB Handbook of British Birds*, 4th edition (Bloomsbury, 2018)

Humble, Kate and McGill, Martin, *Watching Waterbirds with Kate Humble and Martin McGill* (Bloomsbury, 2018)

Taylor, Marianne, *RSPB British Birdfinder* (Bloomsbury, 2018)

SEABIRD CITIES

British Trust for Ornithology *Birds of Conservation Concern 5: The status of all regularly occurring birds in the UK, Channel Islands and the Isle of Man* (British Trust for Ornithology, 2021)

Nicholson, Adam and Boxer, Kate, *The Seabird's Cry – The Lives and Loves of Puffins, Gannets and other Ocean Voyagers* (William Collins, 2017)

Svensson, L, Mullarney, K and Zetterström, D, *Collins Bird Guide*, 3rd edition (Collins, 2022)

Taylor, Marianne, *RSPB Handbook of Seabirds* (Bloomsbury, 2014)

SEAL PUPS

DAERA, *The Wild Seals of Rathlin Island* (DAERA Marine and Fisheries Division, 2019)

Dipper, Francis, *RSPB Spotlight: Seals* (Bloomsbury, 2021)

Duck, Callan, *Seals: Naturally Scottish*, Sea Mammal Research Unit, NatureScot (Scottish Natural Heritage, 2007)

Mammal Society, The, *Seal factsheets*, 'Grey Seal and Harbour Seal' (The Mammal Society, 2022)

ONLINE RESOURCES

The following websites were also useful when researching this guide. Website addresses change occasionally so please use a search engine to find any of interest. See the websites of individual destinations too, for the latest information on opening times and sightings.

Introduction

BBC Weather (bbc.co.uk/weather)
Discover Northern Ireland (discovernorthernireland.com)
Environment Agency (gov.uk/government/organisations/environment-agency)
Gov UK (gov.uk)
Met Office (metoffice.gov.uk)
National Tidal and Sea Level Facility (ntslf.org)
Natural Resources Wales (naturalresources.wales)
Nature's Calendar (naturescalendar.woodlandtrust.org.uk)
NI Direct (nidirect.gov.uk)
RNLI (rnli.org)
SEPA (sepa.org.uk)
Time and Date (timeanddate.com)
Visit Britain (visitbritainshop.com)
Visit Scotland (visitscotland.com)
Visit Wales (visitwales.com)
Woodland Trust (woodlandtrust.org.uk)

Space

American Meteor Society (amsmeteors.org)
Aurora Watch UK (aurorawatch.lancs.ac.uk)
British Astronomical Association (britastro.org)
The Astronomical Society of Edinburgh (astronomyedinburgh.org)
International Meteor Organization (imo.net)
NASA (nasa.gov)

NOAA (Space Weather Enthusiasts Dashboard) (swpc.noaa.gov)
Royal Observatory, Royal Museums Greenwich (rmg.co.uk/royal-observatory)
Time and Date (timeanddate.com)

Weather

British Hang Gliding and Paragliding Association (bhpa.co.uk)
British Gliding Association (gliding.co.uk)
Discovering Britain (discoveringbritain.org)
Met Office (metoffice.gov.uk)
Mountain Weather Information Service (mwis.org.uk)
Perlan Project (perlanproject.org)
Royal Meteorological Society (rmets.org)
World Meteorological Organization (cloudatlas.wmo.int/en/home.html)

Tides

Arnside & Silverdale AONB (arnsidesilverdaleaonb.org.uk)
Caerlaverock Community Association (caerlaverock.org.uk)
Crowle Community Forum (crowle.org)
Guide over Sands Trust (guideoversands.co.uk)
National Tidal and Sea Level Facility (ntslf.org)
National Trust (nationaltrust.org.uk)
North Tyneside Council (my.northtyneside.gov.uk)

Northumberland Coast AONB
(northumberlandcoastaonb.org)
Northumberland County Council
(northumberland.gov.uk)
RNLI (rnli.org)
Rob Bridges YouTube channel
(youtube.com/channel/
UCPKwl1htpSSGieEnJPzkDmw)
States of Guernsey (gov.gg)
The Corryvreckan Whirlpool
(whirlpool-scotland.co.uk)
The Falls of Lora Information
(fallsoflora.info)
The Friends of Hilbre Island
(hilbreisland.info)
The National Coastwatch Institution
(nci.org.uk)
The Severn Bore: A Natural Wonder
of the World (severn-bore.co.uk)
The Severn Bore: Surfers and
Spectators (thesevernbore.co.uk)
Time and Date (timeanddate.com)
Tom Bennett Outdoors
(tombennettoutdoors.co.uk)

Land

British Deer Society (bds.org.uk)
Countryside Code (gov.uk/government/
publications/the-countryside-code)
Discover Scottish Gardens
(discoverscottishgardens.org)
Isle of Rum Red Deer Project
(rumdeer.bio.ed.ac.uk)
Kew Gardens Plants of the World
Online (kew.org)
National Garden Scheme (ngs.org.uk)
National Trust (nationaltrust.org.uk)
Nature's Calendar (naturescalendar
.woodlandtrust.org.uk)
Perth and Kinross Countryside Trust
(pkct.org)
Perthshire Big Tree Country (pkct.org/
pages/category/perthshire-big-tree-
country)

Royal Botanic Garden Edinburgh
(rbge.org.uk)
Royal Forestry Society (rfs.org.uk)
Royal Parks (royalparks.org.uk)
RSPB (rspb.org.uk)
The Mammal Society (mammal.org.uk)
The Woodland Trust (woodlandtrust
.org.uk)
Wildlife Trusts (wildlifetrusts.org)

Water

Anglian Water Services
(anglianwater.co.uk)
Atlantic Salmon Trust
(atlanticsalmontrust.org)
British Dam Society (britishdams.org)
British Hydrological Society
(hydrology.org.uk)
British Mountaineering Council
(thebmc.co.uk)
National Trust (nationaltrust.org.uk)
Philiphaugh Estate (philiphaughestate
.com)
The Association of British and Irish
Show Caves (visitunderground.com)
World of Waterfalls (world-of-
waterfalls.com)

Coast

British Trust for Ornithology (bto.org)
Cumbria Wildlife Trust
(cumbriawildlifetrust.org.uk)
Joint Nature Conservation Committee
(JNCC) (jncc.gov.uk)
RSPB (rspb.org.uk)
Scottish Wildlife Trust
(scottishwildlifetrust.org.uk)
Seal Protection Action Group
(sealaction.org)
The Wildlife Trusts (wildlifetrusts.org)
Wader Quest (waderquest.net)
Wildfowl & Wetlands Trust
(wwt.org.uk)

SPECTACLE SIGHTING RECORD

Chapter		Notes	Sighting 1		Sighting 2		Sighting 3		Sighting 4		Sighting 5	
			Date	Location	Date	Location	Date	Location	Date	Location	Date	Location
SPACE	Meteor showers	Include name of shower										
	Eclipses and supermoons	Fireball										
		Lunar eclipse										
		Solar eclipse										
		Supermoon										
	Northern Lights	Aurora borealis										
		Noctilucent clouds										
WEATHER	Hidden currents	Thunderstorm										
		Inversion										
		Valley fog										
	Mountain clouds	Lenticular clouds										
		Cap or banner cloud										
	Named winds and weather	Helm Cloud and Bar										
		Incoming sea fog / The Haar										
TIDES	Tidal bores	Include name of tidal bore										
	Tidal races	Include name of tidal race										

	Low tide walks	Include name of walk										
LAND	**Autumn colours**	Native species										
		Imported species										
		Champion tree										
	Wildflower displays	Snowdrops										
		Bluebells										
		Cherry blossom										
	Rutting deer	Red/fallow/sika deer										
		Roe deer										
WATER	**Salmon runs**	Waterfall										
		Weir or fish pass										
	Sunken villages	Sunken village										
		Prehistoric forest										
	Wild waterfalls	Spillway flow										
		Spraybow										
		Underground waterfall										
COAST	**Whirling waterbirds**	Wading birds										
		Geese										
	Seabird cities	Cliff site										
		Island site										
	Seal pups	Grey seals										
		Common seals										

INDEX

ACKNOWLEDGEMENTS

When researching this book, the online resources, books and reports listed under 'Further reading' were a great help, as were the many information panels at museums, nature reserves and tourist attractions.

Particular thanks also to the following people for checking extracts of text or figure captions and/or allowing photographs to be used: Matt Clark, Ilona Harris (Weald & Downland Living Museum), Greg Hamerton (Fly with Greg), Kate Lewthwaite (Woodland Trust), Mark Phillips (Astronomical Society of Edinburgh), Nicola Platts (RSPB Snettisham), Patti Purcell (Kielder Observatory Astronomical Society), Sam Robinson (Cairngorm Astronomy Group), Scottish Gliding Centre, Kim Smakes (RSPB Bempton Cliffs), Caitlin Watson (Royal Geographical Society with IBG) and Joanne Wilson (Guide over Sands Trust). Many thanks also to the following people whose words appear in the text: Ian Barthorpe (red deer at RSPB Minsmere), Tom Bennett (the Broomway), Rob Bridges (watching tidal bores), Peter Caton (visiting tidal islands), Sant Cervantes (flying gliders in mountain wave), Matt Clark (weather photography), Kevin Holland (Wiggenhall Wave), Joanna Peaker and Sheila Corcoran (Montrose Basin) and Mark Phillips (meteor watching and photography).

And finally, and most important of all, thanks to Liz Multon at Bloomsbury for saying yes to starting on the marvellous adventure of writing this book and guidance throughout, and Lindsay for her support and enthusiasm for the journey. Many thanks also to my editor Kate Beer, designer Austin Taylor, illustrator Louise Turpin and cartographer John Plumer for producing such a stunning design for the book.